STORYTELLING STEP BY STEP

Marsh Cassady

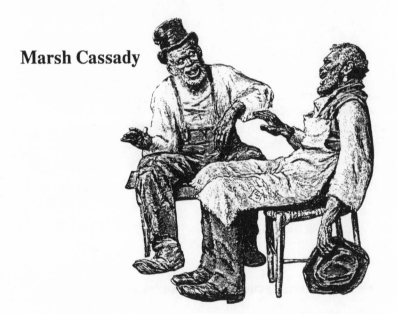

RESOURCE PUBLI
San Jose, Ca

Editorial director: Kenneth Guentert
Production editor: Kathi Drolet
Art director: Terry Ysseldyke-All
Copyediting and production: Elizabeth J. Asborno

Resource Publications, Inc.
160 E. Virginia St., #290
San Jose, CA 95112-5848

Library of Congress Cataloging in Publication Data

Cassady, Marshall.
  Storytelling step by step / Marsh Cassady.
     p. cm.
  Includes bibliographcial references and index.
  ISBN 0-89390-183-0 : $9.95
  1. Storytelling. 2. Title.
LB 1042.C29 1990   90-37986
808.5'43--dc20   CIP

5 4 3 | 94 93

In memory of my grandfathers:
George B. "Clell" Cassady,
who told the best stories a boy ever heard,
and John P. Spahn,
who took me fishing;
and in memory of my grandmothers:
Bertha Eichelberger Spahn,
who once ignored the pain of a broken hip
just so she could see me,
and Barbara Bisbing Cassady,
whom I never was priveleged to know

Contents

INTRODUCTION

I loved to go to my grandfather's house on Sunday afternoons. I remember it so well: the kitchen where we always sat because no other part of the house was ever used, except the bedrooms where Grandpa and Uncle John slept. Grandma had died long before I was born.

There was the old woodburning stove, the oilcloth-covered table, the worn linoleum on the floor. The dark, rich wood of the firewood box was used as a seat for two or three people.

Although I'm sure he wore other clothes, I remember my grandfather (an old man even when I was a kid) always in a flannel shirt, gray work pants with suspenders, clodhopper shoes and a white beard—short in summer, long in winter.

Dad was the youngest surviving child out of sixteen; another had died at birth, a brother Ben drowned when he was eleven or twelve. When I was born, Grandpa already was in his seventies. So, in ways, we seemed separated by more than a couple of generations.

Maybe this and the farm where he lived provided part of the enchantment. It was all so different from my own life that it provided almost a sense of "otherness," an alien quality.

Uncle John, who was already retired from teaching when I first became aware of such things, and Grandpa rarely left the farm, even though earlier in his lifetime Grandpa had roamed the woods of Western Pennsylvania on into the mountains of

1

Maryland, hunting ginseng. And, oh, the wonderful stories he told—of the time he slept beside a log 'way back in the woods and woke up to see a bear sleeping on the other side, or of the time he was bitten by a copperhead snake.

Grandpa would sometimes be gone for months at a time in winter, leaving Grandma alone with the brood of kids. One time he came home in early spring, the trees just beginning to bud, and it was late at night. He'd sold his whole winter's supply of ginseng and had money to last all through the summer till the crops came in. It was late at night, and he decided he'd better hide all the money, so no one would steal it. He lifted the plate on the old iron stove and shoved the money way back inside. Then he went up to his bedroom on the third floor and climbed in beside Grandma, not even waking her. Nestled under quilts and blankets, he didn't know that the night turned cold, that snow began to fall, in big fluffy flakes.
Worn out from his winter's work, resting in the comfort of his sagging bed after sleeping all winter in the woods or in lean-tos, Grandpa was lost to the world. He wasn't even aware that Barbara, his wife, got up at four to make breakfast for all the kids and to have the house warm for them, that she took wood from the firebox, whittled shavings, struck a match, and burned up all the money Grandpa had spent the winter making.

I heard many a tale involving old man Nelson, the man who raised Grandpa when his own parents died; the stagecoach that ran between Somerset and Bedford, Pennsylvania, driven by Grandpa's stepfather; the struggles, defeats, and victories in Grandpa's life.

Hearing these stories was better than going to the movies or listening to the radio. Grandpa was a storyteller. He had the ability to make anything he told interesting. He had dozens, hundreds, maybe even thousands of stories, none that I remember ever repeated. And I sat there enthralled.

My other grandpa told stories too—about how he had to run his family's farm when he was only nine, about working in the coal mine when he was eleven; about the time his dad wanted to teach him to swim and threw him into the Hopewell dam. And how he almost drowned, and how Great-grandpa had to dive in and save him. And how ever after that he wouldn't go near water except to cast a fishing line or take a bath in an old round tub.

Dad told stories too, about the time he came across the woman walking down a country road, the temperature below zero, she dressed in a thin coat and blue from the cold. Her teeth chattered and she could barely speak when he stopped to pick her up, and she didn't know who she was or where she was going, she was so cold.

He told about the time he became so angry at a friend that he threw a dustpan at him in the one-room schoolhouse they attended. And how the friend ducked and the dustpan neatly sliced off all the pages of the calendar on the wall behind where the friend stood.

And I tell stories about the time when life was more innocent and less complicated. When Grandpa Spahn took me fishing and what I hooked was a new fishing pole someone had lost. About the time he took me for an ice-cream cone and stopped to play a pinball machine and I made it squeal "tilt" and felt I'd ruined everything. But Grandpa just laughed and put in another nickel.

I adapt some of the stories I've been told and make them my own: embellishing, adding to, making them not less truthful but more so. Because the funny thing is about stories, no matter how you change them, if you really care, you can't make them untruthful. Stories are more than life; once they're told, they belong to everyone. Yet no one else can take them. Because each teller is different. Each adds his or her own personality, and the stories illustrate not only specific truths as related to the teller, but universal truths as well.

So I tell about how my Grandpa Cassady became separated from his brothers and sisters when he was a little boy and how he wondered all his life what happened to them but never found out. I tell about this little kid, my Grandpa Spahn, who had such a big responsibility when he was only nine because his own father had to work on the railroad to provide money for the younger kids' shoes and clothing.

I tell about this same Grandpa who worked and worked to teach me how to whistle, and when I did, I so startled myself that

I must have jumped a foot. I tell about the time my grandpa accidentally broke the 78-rpm record I'd been wanting for months, just after I'd gotten it. And how bad he felt and how bad I felt.

I tell about the time Dad found the footprints of some prehistoric animal in two rocks in the stream of Grandpa Cassady's farm, and what I think that beast may have been like, and how it roamed the hills. And how it might have been the last of its kind and how lonely it felt until at last it climbed to the highest hill, trumpeting its sorrow and despair to the skies, till at last it sank for the final time to its knees.

I remember reading years ago about a study in which preschoolers watched a TV show and heard a story. Then they were asked which they liked better. They overwhelmingly chose the story. Why? Because on television everything was so cut-and-dried. Listening to a story, they could add their backgrounds, their imaginations, and their fantasies to what they heard.

Maybe I was fortunate, then, to grow up in the age before television. Or at least when TV wasn't so common, and though neighbors and friends had Philcos with rounded screens, we didn't. Maybe that's why I'd much rather hear or write or read or tell stories than watch them on television.

1. THE STORY AND THE TELLER

WHAT IS STORYTELLING?

What exactly are stories, and what does storytelling involve? As implied in the introduction, stories are wondrous magic. They transport us to other worlds, into other lives, into situations we might never encounter ourselves. And yet they are universal. They express common truths, beliefs, yearnings, goals. And the teller herself, himself, is magic. Because this person goes beyond self into mystical realms where anything is real. The teller spins webs of intrigue, of beauty more beauteous than anything we've seen, of sadness so intense it cannot be borne.

These are the sorts of things the entity called story/teller accomplishes. Why "story/teller"? Because they cannot be separated. The story is the teller is the story/teller. Unlike the printed word, a story that is told cannot be recorded accurately on paper. So much depends on other things—on the background of the teller, on the interpretation of emotions, on the way a listener responds, on the state of the teller's thoughts, perceptions, feelings. On the teller's abilities.

Technically, prosaically, story/telling or storytelling can be defined as **an oral art form that provides a means of preserving and transmitting ideas, images, motives, and emotions that are universal.** But rather than that, I prefer to think of storytelling as pure magic. Unfortunately, that doesn't quite suffice as far as analyzing what occurs when a story/teller event is in progress.

Let's take the definition and break it down.

Oral Tradition

First, storytelling is an oral tradition. It's probably safe to say that there were storytellers long before there was written language. So when we think of storytelling, we need to think of something that involves a person using spoken language.

Art Form

Second, it's an art form, although often we don't think of that as being the case. The kind of stories that enthralled me as a young boy, I'm certain, came about naturally without my grandfathers or father thinking in terms of art. But storytelling is similar to other temporal art forms in that the art occurs during the presentation. It cannot exist without the presentation, which it encompasses.

Theatre, dance, music, storytelling—all are similar in that they cannot exist in an unchanging state. A script for a play is not the theatrical production. Pages of music are not a concert. A written story is not a storytelling event. Of course, we can enjoy reading music or a script or a story meant to be told. But they are incomplete in themselves.

Before we go further, it should be mentioned that there is or can be a difference between stories in magazines or fiction anthologies and stories that are told.

Storytelling comes from a folk tradition where people did not rely so much on the written word as they do today. Many people, in fact, couldn't read or had no access to printed material. So they told stories, often with more archetypal characters, often personifying certain traits or characteristics. Generally, these stories involved more clear-cut differences between good and evil. They relied less on long descriptive passages and more on narration or getting the story told.

Of course, the division is only arbitrary. There are some written stories that have less description than told stories. And, of course, written stories can be adapted and told. But, generally, the two forms differ.

A Means of Preserving Images

Our definition also states that storytelling is a means of "preserving" images. This is important in that storytelling does go back for hundreds of years. Many of the same stories told today are simply contemporary adaptations of those that are as ancient as the civilizations of the world. Many are myths or folktales that still have the power to compel the listener's attention. The images are preserved. But like any living art form, storytelling has to change to be applicable to our own time and place.

For years, it seemed, the art was pretty much dying out, except where families gathered to relive their own histories. Then kids heard about the time when Uncle Henry awoke one morning to find his barn burned down and his horses scattered; when Great-grandpa Cassady had a narrow escape from a grizzly bear.

In recent years, however, there has been a resurgence of interest. Why is this? Perhaps, in part, because people are tiring of having their entertainment totally preplanned, slick and packaged. Storytelling does preserve images. But more than that, it *transmits* them.

This means that no storyteller will present his or her art form exactly like any other. When we take an image and make it ours, we adapt and change it. My experiences are different from yours. Yours are different from your aunt's or your neighbor's. You experience a "telling" and add your own background to it. When you retell the story, you relate it more fully to what sort of person you are, to the things that have influenced you.

You make adjustments and improvements. The world changes so that we cannot precisely relate to experiences our great-great-grandparents had. Then we take their experiences, their views of life, and change them to conform more to our present world. And so storytelling preserves through changing. And this is good; it means storytelling is a vibrant, living art.

Universal

In our definition we talked not only about images, but about "ideas," "motivations," and "emotions" that are universal. This means they relate to all of us. Certainly, it can be argued that nothing is totally universal. Yet, the purpose of any art form is sharing. The purpose of storytelling, like any other art form, is to entertain, to present knowledge, to teach behavior and morals. Consider the parables told by Jesus. Entertaining? Yes, but with a far deeper significance.

Stories are used in secular and religious education to illustrate truths and teach the listeners something important about life and how it should be lived. But the teaching is done in a "painless," entertaining way. Because of this, it can make more of an impression. Because stories are interesting, we remember them. How often have you heard a joke—the "story" at its most basic—and could hardly wait to pass it on?

Stories show us how others feel and, in effect, say, "See, if others feel this way, you can too and it's OK." People become angry; they love; they fear; they despise. These emotions are fine; it's what you do with them that's important. "Look, here's what the person in the story does with a particular emotion," the storyteller says. "Is this the proper way to handle the emotion? Is this the way you would handle it?"

A story paints a picture. It uses rhythmic patterns, is pleasing to listen to, is enjoyable and educational. At its best it goes beyond truth in that it illustrates life and so is bigger than life.

WHAT IS A STORYTELLER?

Although there is a wide diversity among the types of people who are storytellers, there are several things they have in common.

First, a storyteller is a person who has a need and a desire to share experiences with others—both direct experiences and acquired ones. This is because, second, a storyteller is a person who likes others and who wants to have direct contact with them.

Third, a storyteller is an entertainer, a ham, someone who truly enjoys telling or performing. But more than that, a storyteller, fourth, interprets life for others.

Storytellers aren't simply content to observe. They want to make sense of their observations. In so doing, they learn and in turn become "social workers" in wanting to share the learning.

They emphasize the significant and teach people a love of language. But they go much beyond language, just as when we type we rarely think of individual keys or even words or sentences. But it's important what these words do, the ideas they convey.

Storytellers try to present truth as they see it. They adhere to the truth of the human condition, of the larger views of life. They have vision, integrity, power to convince and sway.

We might then define a storyteller as a person who helps self and audience enter into other realities both for play/enjoyment and to gain insight and understanding.

The stories storytellers create are a microcosm that show us life "small" but imply a shift outward to a larger reality.

WHY TELL STORIES?

To Release Creativity

In all forms of art, people create because they can't help it. Creativity is a need to express yourself, to say: "Here I am!" It can be a way of explaining things to yourself and making sense of life, of questioning the ways of the world. It's an enlargement of life and a liberation from the prosaic. Like the child, the creative person often creates to understand.

In any art form, there is a joyfulness in bringing an idea to completion. Since a story will not be the same from one time to any other, when we tell, we constantly create. So we can experience the joyfulness at each separate creation.

To Share Experiences

More than that, creation in general and storytelling in particular provide a way to give expression to our experiences, to share them with others. We share direct experiences, taking something from our lives, enlarging it, and presenting it in a telling. Or we take a story we've heard or read, adapt it, and present it because we enjoyed it or because it was particularly meaningful for us.

Often, a story we've read or a happening from our own lives has moved us deeply, and we want to share this with others. So we tell the story to them, and hope they are as moved as we are.

Not only misery loves company, but every other emotion does as well. In this respect, then, storytelling is a sharing of what's in our hearts as well as our intellect.

We tell stories to see that we are similar to others and that they are similar to us. Since this is the case, there is a special bond created, a joyous relationship, between teller and audience. In the best of circumstances, it inspires confidence between one and the other. We feel closer to one another, either as teller with audience or audience with teller. There is a relaxed feeling, a restfulness. Much of this is due to a feeling of "rightness," of belonging.

When engaged in storytelling, we feel a sense of heightened awareness, a high much as runners sometimes experience after several miles. We feel completely and gloriously alive.

Years ago, when I was doing a lot of acting, I often had the feeling that the only true life for me occurred onstage between 8 and 11 p.m. The rest was just filler, something to get through till I could truly be alive. Those engaged in any temporal art can feel the same way.

Often I tell people I'm a ham; what I mean, without spelling it out, is that I love the feeling it gives me to share, to be responsible for starting, continuing, and bringing to completion something that exists only for the moment and in front of an audience.

To Learn

We tell stories to learn about ourselves and our own priorities. By adapting and telling a story, we learn what we like, what influences us, what is most important in our lives. Even more so, we then have a need to share what we've learned with others. Preparing and telling a story helps us to think, to imagine. And when we imagine, we need have no bounds.

Besides helping to know self, telling stories helps us to understand cultures, societies, values, and mores. If we tell nonoriginal stories—that is, stories first told by another person—by the very fact of working closely with them, we catch glimpses into others' minds and ways of thinking. Thus we broaden our own lives. As mentioned, telling stories gives us insights into ourselves. But just as important, it can help listeners make discoveries about themselves and their thinking.

To Pass On History

Often the types of stories we tell help us restructure our experiences and so pass them on. I would suppose that any one of these reasons applied to my Grandpa Cassady's telling of stories. Their telling forced him to rethink what had happened, and in the rethinking, he gained insights (probably unconsciously) into the kind of man he was. In other words, storytelling shows us the truth of who and why we are. This is the case even in telling stories that did not originate with us. When we look at our choices, we can begin to understand why we chose the stories we did, whereas other people's tellings are entirely different, both in selection and presentation.

To Teach

There are also a number of more prosaic reasons for telling stories, particularly to young audiences. First, stories encourage good listening.

Second, children who listen to stories improve their language skills. It has been found that they have an easier time inferring what unfamiliar words mean in the context of an oral story rather than a written one.

Told stories generally have more impact on kids than written stories. As a result, the children remember them better.

11

Told stories give listeners practice in visualization, since, of course, description is created only through spoken words, and each of us adds differing backgrounds to these words to come up with our idea of a character's or setting's appearance.

The storyteller keeps cultural history alive and teaches insight into other people's motivations and behavior. The listeners can appreciate, then, the true "oneness" of human beings.

Finally, children who hear stories often in turn view "literature" as positive and are motivated to read. All in all, they have a more positive attitude about books and the written word.

THE STORY / TELLER / LISTENER RELATIONSHIP

What is storytelling, then? It is an event, involving at least two people—a sender and a receiver—each of whom pays attention to and therefore affects the other. It uses its own special conventions, devices, and effects, different from any other art form.

It has been said that in the best theatrical performance, it's impossible to separate the actor from the role. This should be even more applicable to storytelling. The teller is, in part, the story. An actor speaks someone else's lines, follows an interpretation made in part by other theatrical artists—the director, the costumer, the set designer.

The storyteller, as stated, adapts and makes the story his own, using his own individual style and method of presentation, yet using the language of the community. Certainly, no one telling a story (unless it's memorized) uses the same language as anyone else. We have to allow for individuality. Yet, the language cannot be far removed from that which is familiar to the audience, or else the storytelling event will be of little consequence.

Storytelling is also a mutual creation between listener and teller. The teller is affected first by the language and lifestyle of the community. Much of this she probably doesn't even consciously consider. She knows the speech of others with whom she associates or will associate. She adapts her speech to this, either consciously or unconsciously.

One of the characters in Tom Wolfe's novel, *Bonfire of the Vanities,* says "He don't" or "She don't" even though he knows this is improper. He uses incorrect grammar because, among those with whom he works, it is expected. Less blatantly, a storyteller does the same thing. He takes what is usual and common, relates it to the story and so presents it.

As in all other forms of temporal art, there is a contract established between the teller and the listener, to which each has responsibilities. The teller agrees to relate the story to the best of his or her abilities; the audience members agree to pay attention and absorb the presentation. There is a shared purpose, that of grasping and understanding, of learning, most certainly of being entertained. For if the teller doesn't like what she's doing, hasn't actually made the story her own, she isn't living up to the contract.

Contracts of any sort sometimes don't work out. The same may be true of the storytelling event. Tellers lose their audiences for any number of reasons: poor location, noise or other interference, the mental state of either the teller or the listener, and so on. But still, each—the teller and the listener—by the very fact of the event's taking place, have the duty to try their best to see that the contract is successful.

You can't separate the teller from the audience. There would be no teller without an audience. There would be no communication. One affects the other. Each must be considerate of the other in the telling. Stories bind people together, not only the teller with the audience, but the teller and audience with the past and with the future. A commonality of experiences concerned with the human being is pointed up, talked about, presented from generation to generation, from century to century. This is storytelling.

Exercises

1. From your own experience or that of a family member, develop a story that you could tell to a particular audience. Decide who will be your audience and the purpose of the story, and then develop the idea accordingly.

2. Think back over stories or anecdotes you've heard. Now take one of these, make it uniquely yours, develop it as fully as you can, and tell it—whether in an actual storytelling setting or to friends or relatives.

3. At the end of this chapter are two folktales—that is, stories whose specific source cannot be traced. Choose one of them, think of an audience to which you might present it, and change and adapt it so that it fits that audience. Learn the story, practice it, and tell it to an audience, whether of one or more people.

4. Go to your library; browse around, looking at collections of fables, myths, and/or folktales. Find several sources that you might use and adapt for future stories. Spend time reading the tales and thinking about which ones you like and why. Choose one or two that you think you might like to tell. Keep them in mind for the future.

5. Think of story/tellers you have experienced. Did you like the presentation? Try to figure out why or why not. Think of the stories and the tellers and try to decide specifically what they did to hold your attention or make it wander. You can choose stories that were told only to you or those that were part of a larger presentation.

PAUL BUNYAN'S BIG GRIDDLE

Once, the king of Sweden drove all the good farmers out of the country and a senator from North Dakota he wanted all the fine upstanding timber cleared off the whole state so as to make room for them, so he asked Paul Bunyan for to do the job, and Paul he took the contract. Paul cut lumber out in North Dakota at the rate of a million foot a hour, and he didn't hardly know how to feed his men, he had so many in the camp. The worst trouble was with his hotcake griddle. It weren't near big enough though it were a pretty good size. The cookees used to grease it with telephone poles with bunches of gunny sacks on the end, but it weren't near big enough. Paul knew where he could get a bigger griddle but he didn't hardly know how to get it to the camp. When it was got up on one aidge it made a track as wide as a wagon road and it were pretty hard to lift. So Paul he thought, and finally he hitched up his mule team. The mule team could travel so fast when they had their regular feed of seven bushels of wheat apiece that nobody couldn't hold them, and Paul had to drive them to a flat-bottomed wagon without no wheels. This time Paul hitched a couple of these here electromagnets on the back, and he drove off to where the griddle was, and he swung them magnets round till he got the griddle on its aidge, and then he drove off lippity-cut to the camp, and he got the griddle a-goin' round so fast he didn't hardly know how to stop it, but he got her near the place where he wanted it, and then he let her go by herself, and she went round and round and round and round, gittin' nearer and nearer the center, and finally she gouged out a hole big enough for a furnace and settled down on top. Then Paul he built a corral around the griddle and put a diamond-shaped roof over it, and built some grain elevators alongside, and put in eight of the biggest concrete mixers he could find. Long in the afternoon every day they'd begin to fill the elevators and start the mixers, and then the cookees would grease the griddle. They all had slabs of bacon on their feet, and they each had their routes. Paul he fixed up a fence of chicken wire round the aidge, in case some cookees didn't get off quick enough when the batter began to roll down, so's they'd have some place to climb to. When the batter was all ready somebody on the aidge used to blow a whistle, and it took four minutes for the sound to get across. Then they'd trip the chute, and out would roll a wave of hotcake batter four feet high, and any poor cookee that was overtook was kinda out of luck.

Paul's cook shanty was so big that he had to have lunch counters all along the wall so's the hands could stop and get something to eat before they found their places or else they'd get faint a-lookin' for them. Paul he had the tables arranged in three decks, with the oldest hands on the top; and the men on the second deck wore tin hats like a fireman's, with little spouts up the back, and away from the third deck Paul ran a V-flume to the pigpen, for Paul he did hate waste. The problem was how to get the grub to the crew fast enough, because the cookees had so far to go from the cook shanty that it all got cold before they could get it on the table. So Paul he put a stop-clock ten foot across the face so as he could see it any place in the eatin' shanty, and he got in one of these here efficiency experts, and they got it all timed down to the plumb limit how long it ought to take to get that food hot to the table. Then Paul he decided to put in some Shetland ponies on roller skates for to draw the food around, and everything seemed fine. But them ponies was trotters, and they couldn't take the corners with any speed, and Paul he had to learn 'em how to pace, and a whole lot of victuals was wasted while he was a-learnin' of them, and Paul was losin' time and he knowed it. So finally he done away with the ponies and put in a train of grub cars with switches and double track and a loop at the end back to the main line, so that when the cars got started proper they came back by themselves. And Paul put in a steel tank especial for the soup, with an air-compressor cupola, six hundred pounds to the square inch, and they used to run the soup down to the men through a four-inch fire hose which the feller on top used to open up as he came through.

WHY THE SEA IS SALT

Once on a time, but it was a long, long time ago, there were two brothers, one rich and one poor. Now, one Christmas Eve, the poor one hadn't so much as a crumb in the house, either of meat or bread, so he went to his brother to ask him for something to keep Christmas with, in God's name. It was not the first time his brother had been forced to help him, and you may fancy he wasn't very glad to see his face, but he said, "If you will do what I ask you to do, I'll give you a whole flitch of bacon."

So the poor brother said he would do anything and was full of thanks.

"Well, here is the flitch," said the rich brother, "and now go straight to hell."

"What I have given my word to do, I must stick to," said the other; so he took the flitch and set off. He walked the whole day, and at dusk he came to a place where he saw a very bright light.

"Maybe this is the place," said the man to himself. So he turned aside, and the first thing he saw was an old, old man, with a long white beard, who stood in a woodshed, hewing wood for the Christmas fire.

"Good even," said the man with the flitch.

"The same to you. Whither are you going so late?" said the man.

"Oh, I'm going to hell, if I only knew the right way," answered the poor man.

"Well, you're not far wrong, for this is hell," said the old man. "When you get inside, they will be all for buying your flitch, for meat is scarce in hell; but mind you don't sell it unless you get the hand-quern which stands behind the door for it. When you come out, I'll teach you how to handle the quern, for it's good to grind almost anything."

So the man with the flitch thanked the other for his good advice, and gave a great knock at the Devil's door.

When he got in, everything went just as the old man had said. All the devils, great and small, came swarming up to him like ants 'round an anthill, and each tried to outbid the other for his flitch.

"Well," said the man, "By rights, my old dame and I ought to have this flitch for our Christmas dinner; but since you all set your hearts on it, I suppose I must give it up to you; but if I sell it at all, I'll have it for that quern behind the door yonder."

At first the Devil wouldn't hear of such a bargain and chaffered and haggled with the man; but the man stuck to what he said, and at last the devil had to part with his quern. When the man got out into the yard, he asked the old woodcutter how he was to handle the quern; and after he had learned how to use it, he thanked the old man and went off home as fast as he could, but still the clock had struck twelve on Christmas Eve before he reached his own door.

"Wherever in the world have you been?" said his old dame. "Here have I sat for hour after hour, waiting and watching, without so much as two sticks to lay together under the Christmas brose."

"Oh," said the man, "I couldn't get back before, for I had to go a long way first for one thing, and then for another; but now you shall see."

So he put the quern on the table and bade it first of all grind lights, then a tablecloth, then meat, then ale, and so on, till they had got everything that was nice for Christmas fare. He had only to speak the work and the quern ground out what he wanted. The old dame stood by blessing her stars and kept on asking where he had got this wonderful quern, but he wouldn't tell her.

"It's all one where I got it from; you see the quern is a good one, and the millstream never freezes. That's enough."

So he ground meat and drink and dainties enough to last out till Twelfth Day, and on the third day he asked all his friends and kin to his house and gave a great feast. Now when the rich brother saw all that was on the table and all that was behind in the larder, he grew quite spiteful and wild, for he couldn't bear that his brother should have anything.

"'Twas only on Christmas eve," he said to the rest, "he was in such straits that he came and asked for a morsel of food in God's name, and now he gives a feast as if he were count or king." And he turned to his brother and said, "But whence, in hell's name, have you got all this wealth?"

"From behind the door," answered the owner of the quern, for he didn't care to let the cat out of the bag. But later on in the evening, when he had got a drop too much, he could keep his secret no longer, and he brought out the quern and said, "There, you see what has gotten me all this wealth!" He made the quern grind all kinds of things. When his brother saw it, he set his heart on having the quern, and, after a deal of coaxing, he got it; but he had to pay three hundred dollars for it, and his brother bargained to keep it till hay harvest, "for," he thought, "if I keep it till then, I can make it grind meat and drink that will last for years." So you may fancy the quern didn't grow rusty for want of work, and when hay harvest came, the rich brother got it, but the other took care not to teach him how to handle it.

It was evening when the rich brother got the quern home, and next morning he told his wife to go out into the hayfield and toss, while the mowers cut the grass, and he would stay at home and get the dinner ready. So, when dinner time drew near, he put the quern on the kitchen table and said, "Grind herrings and broth, and grind them good and fast."

So the quern began to grind herrings and broth; first of all, all the dishes full, then all the tubs full, and on till the kitchen floor was quite covered. The man twisted and twisted at the quern to get it to stop, but for all his twisting and fingering, the quern went right on grinding, and in a little while the broth rose so high that he was like to drown. So he threw open the kitchen door and ran into the parlor, but it wasn't long before the quern had ground the parlor full too, and it was only at the risk of his life that the man could get hold of the latch of the house door through the stream of broth. When he got the door open, he ran out and set off down the road, with the stream of herrings and broth at his heels, roaring like a waterfall over the whole farm.

Now his old dame, who was tossing hay in the field, thought it a long time to dinner, and at last she said, "Well, though the master doesn't call us home, we may as well go. Maybe he finds it hard work to boil the broth and will be glad of my help."

The men were willing enough, so they sauntered homeward, but just as they had got a little way up the hill, what should they meet but herrings, and broth, and bread, all running and dashing and splashing together in a stream, and the master himself running before them for his life. As he passed them he bawled out, "Would to heaven each of you had a hundred throats! But take care you're not drowned in the broth!"

Away he went, as though the Evil One were at his heels, to his brother's house and begged him, for God's sake, take back the quern that instant, for, said he, "If it grinds only one hour more, the whole parish will be swallowed up by herrings and broth."

But his brother wouldn't hear of taking it back till the other paid him down three hundred dollars more.

So the poor brother got both the money and the quern, and it wasn't long before he set up a farmhouse far finer than the one in which his brother lived and with the quern he ground so much gold that he covered his house with plates of gold; and as the farm lay by the seaside, the golden house gleamed and glistened far away over the sea. All who sailed by put ashore to see the rich man in the golden house and to see the wonderful quern, the fame of which spread far and wide, till there was nobody who hadn't heard tell of it.

So one day there came a skipper who wanted to see the quern, and the first thing he asked was if it could grind salt.

"Grind salt!" said the owner. "I should just think it could. It can grind anything."

When the skipper heard that, he said he must have the quern, cost what it would, for if he only had it, he thought he should be rid of his long voyage across stormy seas for a lading of salt.

Well, at first the man wouldn't hear of parting with the quern; but the skipper begged and prayed so hard that at last he let him have it, but he had to pay many, many thousand dollars for it.

Now when the skipper had got the quern on his back, he soon made off with it, for he was afraid lest the man would change his mind; so he had not time to ask how to handle the quern but got on board his ship as fast as he could and set sail.

When he had sailed a good way off, he brought the quern out on deck and said, "Grind salt, and grind both good and fast."

Well, the quern began to grind salt so that it poured out like water, and when the skipper had got the ship full, he wished it to stop the quern, but whichever way he turned it and however much he tried, it was no good; the quern kept grinding on, and the heap of salt grew higher and higher, and at last, down sunk the ship.

And so, there lies the quern at the bottom of the sea and grinds away at this very day, and that's why the sea is salt.

2. AUDIENCE AND LOCATION

When you plan to tell a story, it is important that you know ahead of time all that you can about the occasion, the audience, and the location, all of which relate to your purpose in the telling.

THE CREATION

I

In the beginnin' of time,
Not your time, nor my time,
But clear at first when things started happenin',
God said to himself,
"I'm gonna have a little fun,
I'm gonna create Me a world."
He reached out his arm and grabbed a hunk of space.
Then He started a-squeezin' and a- squeezin'
Till you thought sure it'd bust;
But purty soon
He got it so tight together
It looked just like a big mud pie,
'Ceptin' it didn't have any shape.
Then He wound up His arm and let fly.
He was a dern good pitcher, too.
The ol' ball o' dirt went clear out into darkness
Away from His shinin' face,
And that was purty doggone far.
Then God set Himself down and thought,
"If this world's gonna amount to anything,
It's gotta have water.
He looked all around and found a squirt gun
One of the little angels had left layin' in the heavenly grass.
He never could get 'em to put away their toys.
So the Lord walked over to the pump
And filled it full.
He took careful aim...and let go.
He hit the target right square in the middle,
And that gun was so powerful
It started the ball a spinnin' right where it had stopped.
But the world was 'way out in darkness,
And God couldn't hardly see it at all.
Then He thought,

"That ain't gonna be any fun if'n I don't see it.
I'm gonna have to make some light."
He went over to the ol' heavenly swamp,
And there He found a dried cat-o'-nine-tail.
He picked it and took it to His garage.
There the Lord dipped it in kerosene and lit it.
He gave a powerful heave
And threw it out, real close to Earth,
Just close enough so's not to melt it.
As the thing flew along,
Some of the seeds dropped out
And kept on a-burnin'.
They was purty,
And God wanted to give 'em a nice name,
So He named 'em stars.
Then He wanted to make another light,
One for the other side of Earth.
He found an ol' shavin' mirror, picked it up,
Spun His arm around—just like a discus thrower—
And let it sail.
It went 'way 'round Earth 'fore it stopped,
And this was the moon.
And even to this day,
We can see God's reflection in it
As he looks down at us.
The Lord was awful tired by this time,
And He went home and hit the hay.

II

The next mornin'
God was so excited
He got up real early.
The first thing He done was decide
He best make it so Earth couldn't see heaven
And so wouldn't be blinded by the sun's reflectin' off
    the golden halos of the angels.
He closed His Lips and blew into His Mouth, hard,
Compressin' His Breath.

Then He blew toward Earth and made clouds.
This took 'most all day.
It wasn't easy blowin' His Breath that far,
And that's about all He got done.

III

But the next day, God got up early again.
He wanted to make Earth beautiful,
Give it a little bit of Heaven.
He gathered up some Heavenly grasses and trees and things,
And got one of the angels,
One with long white wings,
To fly over the world and scatter 'em around
So they'd grow.
And God said to the angel,
"If any o' that water gets in the way,
Just make a dam or scrape the mud away with your fingernail
And let it run in that."
The angel sure had a lot of fun,
Plantin' and plannin' where things'd look best.
The short green plants with the sharp needles
On the flat parts,
The trees with the less sharp needles
On the mounds
And everything else where it looked the nicest.
The angel spent a lot o' time,
Just 'bout all day.
God knew it'd be too late to try anything else,
So He waited till the next new day.

IV

God plum forgot about all he had to do in Heaven, though,
Like leadin' choir practice and holdin' angel scout meetin' and
    so forth,
So He didn't get much done with Earth.
All he done was figure out how to fix the weather
So's it wouldn't get so monotonous.
He figured he'd install a sprinkler system outside His house.

When Earth got dry, He'd turn it on.
When it was too wet, He'd turn it off.
Later, He left it up to some angels,
And sometimes they forgot all about it.
It almost burned up, and once,
They just 'bout ruinated the whole world
'Cause they forgot to turn it off.
Then the Lord thought,
"I better make it so Earth can have some temperature changes."
He found an old 'lectric heater
And pointed it toward the world.
When it was turned on, it was summer.
When He shut it off, it was winter.
When it was coolin' down, that was fall,
And when He was waitin' for it to get real warm,
That there was spring.

V

The next day God really had fun.
He took a little chunk from the Earth—
Which made the Grand Canyon—
And made some live things.
They were all sorts of shapes and sizes.
Some even had wings like the angels.He worked all day,
And finally finished makin' the animals 'way late at night.
Since He was so tired, He went to bed.
He wanted to try to finish next day.

VI

God decided He better make something big,
Something to be in charge of everything else,
So He made Man.
Since Man was to have so much responsibility,
God was extra careful
And found the nicest piece of dirt there was,
And decided to shape Man just a little different from Himself
    and the angels.
He formed Man,

26

Blew His Own Breath into him
And he lived.
Then God left man alone,
But purty soon, man called,
"God, I'm lonesome.
Can't you make something else like me,
Something I can talk to and'll understand me?"
So God thought and decided to create woman.
He was a good surgeon
And He gave the man some ether
And put him to sleep.
He cut out the man Adam's rib and made a woman called Eve.
God was all tuckered out
And He went back to Heaven and slept.

VII

The only thing God done next day
Was get up early
And bless His work
And say that it was good.
Then He set in His easy chair by the fireplace
And rested.
His work was finished
And he had made the world.

With this poem I took a familiar story from the Bible and presented it almost like a folktale. Such a story could be told under many different circumstances and for a lot of different audiences. Before you tell the story, however, you need to think about the audience and the occasion.

First, what is the age group of the audience? Adults, teenagers, small children, or mixed? You need to analyze what is unique about them. This, more than likely, is tied in to the purpose of meeting. The way you introduce the story and end the presentation bear directly on your purpose.

"The Creation" could be presented simply for entertainment to adults or children or to a mixed audience, or it could be a painless way of teaching the creation story to children. It's also the type of story that can be easily adapted to fit the teller's background and personality.

As it is written here, the persona of the narrator comes through strongly as formally uneducated but definitely not lacking in intelligence. If you feel uncomfortable with the deliberately incorrect grammar, you can change it.

STORYTELLING OCCASIONS

When is it appropriate to tell stories? What kinds of stories do different age groups like? How long should your stories be?

Stories can be told almost any time people congregate. Stories are used as parts of speeches and as ways of teaching classes. When families gather for weddings or funerals or reunions, one of the major activities is telling family stories. They usually start with: "Do you remember the time...?"

Stories are told for holidays like Christmas or Halloween or Independence Day.

No matter what the occasion, however, you have to keep your audience in mind. Young kids, those in the primary grades, generally like short, simple stories. One such as "The Rescue" can be used to teach the need to respect others' freedoms and ways of life.

THE RESCUE
by Pat Cassady

Last summer a little chipmunk lived in a hollow log at the edge of the woods.

The Spencer family lived in a big, brick house close by. A stone wall separated their lawn from the woods.

One day the chipmunk was running along the wall when "plop," a soft paw came down on him and held him fast. A large, yellow cat had caught him. He wiggled and wiggled but could not get free.

Just then, Susan, a little girl who lived in the house, opened the door and began calling, "Kitty, kitty, kitty. Come and get your lunch." The yellow cat just stared at her with his big, green eyes, then pushed down a little harder on the chipmunk's back.

When Susan saw what was happening, she ran quickly to the wall. "Let go," she yelled. "Let go of him right now." The cat would not.

"Daddy, daddy," she called. "Come here! Please! Hurry!"

Daddy came outside. "What's going on here?" he asked. Then he saw. In no time at all he was holding the large, yellow cat with one hand and freeing the tiny chipmunk with the other.

"We'll take him into the house for a while to see if he is hurt," Daddy said. He was holding the chipmunk with one hand on top and one on the bottom. Susan saw that the chipmunk was shivering.

When they got to the house, Susan ran to get a little box for the chipmunk. Daddy put it into the box, and it was very still for a while.

"It looks OK to me," said Daddy. "Just scared, I guess."

"May I keep him, please, may I, Daddy? I would take good care of him. Please!"

Daddy picked Susan up very slowly, gave her a squeeze, and said, "No, sweetheart, I'm afraid not. Well, maybe just one night. Little wild animals need to be in the woods where they can be free and can get the right kind of food and have their own friends."

The next morning Susan and Daddy took the chipmunk to the woods. They walked far back among the trees. Susan carried the box and Daddy carried the hollow log that was the tiny chipmunk's home.

"Now the cat won't find him again," Daddy said. He put the log on the ground among the bushes.

"Good-bye," Susan said as she turned the box on its side and let the chipmunk scamper away. Then she put her hand in Daddy's hand, and they walked back to the house.

Children from ten through early teens are particularly interested in folktales and myths. They also might be interested in stories about life in earlier generations. The story on the next page is an example.

THRESHING DAY
by Pat Cassady

Patty, breakfast is ready," Grandma called from the foot of the stairs. The faint odor of pancakes drifted up along with her voice. I sat up in bed, stretched, yawned, and rubbed my eyes in the bright summer sunshine that shone through the bedroom window. Then I rolled over, groaned, and was about to take another nap when the grinding of steel wagon wheels on the hard dirt road reminded me. Today was not just another day on the farm. Threshing day had finally come. The threshing machine was already arriving. Hurriedly, I jumped into my jeans and shirt, ran downstairs, gulped down a buckwheat cake and was off to do the chores.

"I shall have to hurry this morning," I thought as I scattered wheat for the chickens. "Since I am eight years old now, maybe I will be allowed to go into the barnyard and watch the workers instead of looking through the garden gate. I will go into the barnyard! If Grandma wants me she can call." Since Daddy, Grandpa, and my two brothers were at the barn and Grandma was busy preparing dinner, I ran down the long, narrow garden walk and through the gate without anyone noticing me.

The threshing machine was sticking its long nose out over the old straw stack. Farmers in their patched and faded overalls and shabby straw hats were walking about, fastening the wide belt from the tractor to the machine, adjusting things, and calling loudly to one another in a mixture of German and English.

Then the big belt suddenly began to go around. I stepped back. The machine made a loud noise as it swallowed the sheaves, blew the chaff from its long nose, and let clean grain run from the pipes on either side. While this was going on, the men were running here and there, pitching sheaves of wheat and oats, and carrying heavy sacks of grain.

The whole procedure fascinated me for a while, but I wanted to get into the act. I looked around for my brothers. Surely, I could do what they were doing. Then I heard them in the granary. Looking through the door, I saw that they were pushing the grain back as the men poured it into the bins. "Please let me get into the bin and help," I pleaded. They agreed to let me in for a few minutes. I worked hard, but every time I pushed some grain toward the back a man would come and pour another sack of wheat in. Sometimes the men almost buried me. I did not mind. The grain felt cool on my bare feet and down my back. Besides, now I had a real part in threshing day.

My ecstasy was short-lived, however, for ten minutes later I heard my name. Grandma was calling to remind me that I was just a girl and had to help in the kitchen. There was no use pretending I had not heard her. Dean and Linn had heard the call and were not at all unhappy to see me leave.

At the house, Grandma thought of the most unpleasant jobs for me to do while she and Aunt Alta prepared the food. Since we used the best dishes and the good silverware only once each year, they got very dusty. My first job was washing these dishes and polishing the silverware. Then I had to set the table, fill the glasses with water, and bring extra chairs down from upstairs.

Soon the men began coming up the garden walk. While they washed off their sweat and dirt in the washpans that Grandma had placed on benches in the backyard, I sat on the porch and watched the threshers. They talked and laughed and pointed to things. I did not know what they said, but it was fun to try to guess.

Then they filed into the dining room and took their places at the long table. Standing at the kitchen door, I breathed in the rich odor of the fried chicken, mashed potatoes, creamed corn, fresh-baked bread and apple pie as Grandma and Aunt Alta carried the food into the men.

"Why do I have to wait until the threshers get finished eating before I can eat? I helped thresh too," I said to myself. The men ate so slowly. They talked and talked between each bite, and they took so many bites!

When the men were finally finished, we women cleared the table, put clean plates on, and ate with the children. We ate like threshers too.

Dinner over, the men went to the barn to prepare to go to the neighboring farms to thresh there. Again I heard the sound of steel wheels grinding on the hard dirt road, but another noise was added. This time the grinding was mingled with the clatter of dishes in my dishpan as I washed and washed and washed.

Young adults seem to enjoy traditional literature most, while adults enjoy many types of stories.

When telling stories to different age groups, it's a good idea to keep probable attention spans in mind. For preschool age children, a program of storytelling should be about twenty minutes. For older kids the number can be doubled, while young adults and adults will be content to listen for up to an hour-and-a-half. But, for programs this long, you should plan a break.

WHERE STORIES ARE TOLD

Stories are often told as part of religious services, rarely by themselves but to illustrate a point the speaker is making. They are told at business lunches, at banquets of all sorts, and at conventions and conferences. Most likely, at these places too, they are part of a larger presentation. Still, they should be given as much attention and care as stories that are to stand by themselves.

There are story hours at most libraries, where either a librarian, a volunteer, or a professional storyteller presents the program. Often libraries ask for volunteer tellers, which is a good way to get started telling stories. And there's nothing wrong with simply going to the library and asking if you can have a chance to tell stories.

Another good place for telling is in the children's wing of a hospital. Sometimes there is a structured program, which you may want to investigate, or again you can call to see about starting a program. More than likely, the hospital will welcome you.

I have told lots of stories to senior citizens groups, on such occasions as monthly meetings, enrichment classes, and banquets. Always, I've found such groups to be highly appreciative and courteous.

Often, retirement homes and nursing homes welcome programs of storytelling. To older groups, the nostalgia story can have a great appeal. But don't make the mistake of thinking that older people, just because they are seniors, like stories featuring only people their own age. Far from it. They like humor, dramatic action, intrigue—really the entire range of oral literature.

A great number of clubs and groups welcome storytellers. Scouting organizations thrive on stories—often, the sillier, the better. A type that might appeal to them is the following, which I heard years ago and have told many times to a variety of groups. Often, this type of story, called a "shaggy dog story," akin to the tall tale, has no reason for existing other than entertainment. The story appears here in abbreviated form. One of the features of a shaggy dog story is that the teller tries to drag it out as long as possible and still hold the readers attention.

WILLIE THE MOTH

You know the reputation moths have for ruining closets full of clothing. Well, the reputation is well deserved. To illustrate my point, I want to tell you about a moth named Willie.

Now Willie was a little guy, not much bigger than a flea, but he had an appetite that went on and on and on. Even when all the other moths settled down to read the latest mystery story or watch television, Willie just kept on eating.

One day, Willie's uncle stopped in for dinner and noticed that after the last burp was concluded and the last chair shoved back under the table, his nephew just sat there continuing to eat—an entire tweed coat, a bulky wool sweater and a feather boa for dessert.

"Say, Willie," Uncle Randolph said, "I heard about a contest that might interest you."

"Muh-wha chomp chomp k-uhuh-inda munch munch con-glugglug-test, muhchompmunch-Uncle munchmunch-Randy?"

"An eating contest."

The announcement got Willie's complete attention. "An eating contest?" he said. "What kind of an eating contest?"

"Well, it starts right in your own closet. All the moth families compete with each other to see who can eat the most at one setting. Whoever wins goes on to the district contest. Then to the state. Then the national contest. And finally, the world contest."

"And all you have to do is eat?" Willie said.

"That's right," Uncle Randy said.

"I'm pretty good at that," said Willie.

Willie's mama and papa and brothers and sisters and uncles and aunts and grandma and grandpa on his mother's side and on his father's side all laughed uproariously. "Indeed you are, Willie," his mama said.

So Willie decided to enter the contest. It was to be held a week from last Thursday. Willie worried about getting in shape. Should he go without food so he'd want more when the contest started? Or should he eat more than usual to try to stretch his stomach? After deliberating for, oh, at least a couple of seconds, Willie chose the latter course, until his mama threatened to send him to the closet in the next bedroom where all the clothes were kept in plastic containers.

On the day of the contest, Willie and his whole family traveled to the other end of the closet for the local contest. Willie was frightened when he noticed that all the other moths who were entering were at least two times bigger than he was. Some even more. Some as big as sparrows and crows and eagles and...

"Don't worry, Willie, you'll do OK," his mama said. "Believe me, I know."

There were ten contestants and a lot of attendants to be certain that no one ran out of delicious woolen underwear and head scarves and topcoats. When all ten moths were in their places behind a long table with gracefully curving legs, and bibs were tied around their necks, the oldest moth there held up a spray gun and fired toward the ceiling. (The gun was full of soda pop, not bug spray.) This was the signal to start eating.

All ten moths did just that. They began eating and eating and eating. And they ate and they ate and they ate. And they were eating and eating and eating and they ate and they ate and they ate, and nobody seemed even close to dropping out. But Willie wasn't worried. After all, he hadn't put anything into his stomach since lunchtime two hours earlier. And then all he'd had were two woolen suits and an old knit hat. So he kept on eating and eating and eating and he ate and he ate and he ate. And all the other moths kept on eating and they ate and they ate and they ate, when suddenly, one moth, a little bigger than Willie, threw a wing over his mouth and ran from the table, his stomach heaving uncontrollably.

The other moths barely gave him a glance. They kept on eating and eating and eating and they ate and they ate and they ate and Willie kept on eating and eating and eating and he ate and he ate and he ate.

And one by one all the other moths began to drop out. Willie wondered why. He still was pretty ravenous himself. So he kept on eating and eating and eating and he ate and he ate and he ate. And the moths that were left kept on eating and eating and eating and they ate and they ate and they ate. And then there were only three of them left.

The one on Willie's left kept on eating and eating and eating. And he ate and he ate and he ate. And the one on Willie's right kept on eating and eating and eating. And he ate and he ate and he ate. And Willie kept on eating and eating and eating. And he ate and he ate and he ate. And the one on his left kept on eating and eating and... Then he looked up, shrugged and left the table. Now there were only two moths left.

The other moth, Big Joe, was the size of an eagle. Willie knew his name was Big Joe because he had it tattooed on his beak. And besides, just like Willie, he had his own cheering section. They kept yelling: "Go, Big Joe, go, go, go. Go, Big Joe, go. Eat and eat and eat and eat. Go, Big Joe, go."

During all of this, Joe kept on eating and eating and eating and he ate and he ate and he ate. And Willie kept on eating and eating and eating and he ate and he ate and he ate. But he was starting to get a little bit worried. His tummy was beginning to feel just the slightest bit full. And all he'd had were seventeen pair of woolen pants, thirteen shirts, five socks and a toothpick. The latter was an accident.

But all the while Joe kept eating and eating and eating and while Willie ate and ate and ate, Willie's family and friends started to feel kind of bad that they didn't have a special cheer like Joe's supporters did. After all, Willie was up there eating and eating and eating, doing his level best. They wanted him to know they were behind him too, just as Joe's contingent was behind him. So they put their heads together, and pretty soon they came up with: "Willie, Willie, don't be silly, it's not chilly, go. Be a dilly, ride a filly, eat those clothes, oh ho."

Well, that was a really dumb cheer, and Willie was a little embarrassed because of it. But he didn't let it slow down his eating and eating and eating. Because he just ate and he ate and he ate. And anyhow, he figured, his cheering section was doing the best it could. Just as he was.

Sooo... [Here you may want to bring in some audience participation by having everyone say:] Willie kept on eating and eating and eating and he ate and he ate and he ate. And Joe... kept on eating and eating and he ate and he ate and he ate.

And now Willie was really getting worried because he had to admit it, the last three sets of elbow patches tasted, well, not as good as they should, even though they were Willie's favorite food next to rolls and rolls of red wool yarn. And even though he kept on eating and eating and eating, and even though he ate and he ate and he ate, he had to admit he was really getting awfully full.

He glanced over at Joe who kept on... eating and eating and eating and he ate and he ate and he ate. And Willie kept on... eating and eating and eating and he ate and he ate and he ate. And suddenly Willie heard this gigantic gulp, and he looked over at Joe, who was gazing right back at him.

"Well, little feller," Joe said. "You beat me fair and square." Because, you see, even though he felt his stomach might burst, Willie still kept on... eating and eating and eating and he ate and he ate and he ate. And then he stopped because he knew he'd won.

The entire closet broke out in cheers and people came by to shake legs and pat Willie's wings. And he was a hero. On the way home to Willie's part of the closet, Uncle Randy mentioned that now, of course, since Willie had won the local contest, he was eligible to go on to district, held in the downstairs closet of the big house next door.

Well, [Without going into lavish detail, though you may want to when you tell the story], at this second contest Willie kept on eating and eating and eating and he ate and he ate, and he won this contest too. The same for the state contest, and the national, even though the other contestants kept getting bigger and bigger and bigger the more important the contest. [This you may also want to investigate further in order to bring all the savory details to your listeners.]

And finally, Willie went to the world contest [which I'm sure your listeners would really want to hear about, but which we'll deal skimpily with here in order to converse space]. By this time he was an old hand at contests, maybe feeling even a little bit too overconfident. But why not? He was the littlest contestant in any of the contests and still he won. So he wasn't worried. He even ordered a pre-contest snack from room service.

Suffice it to say that again Willie kept on eating and eating and eating and he ate and he ate and he ate while all the other contestants kept on eating and eating and eating and they ate and they ate and they ate. Poor Willie didn't think anyone would ever drop out. But [you, as storyteller, provide the details] one by one they did, until again only Willie and one gigantic moth were left. Of course, by this time with all the food he'd eaten, Willie was much bigger himself, almost as big as a horsefly now. And he still hadn't lost any of his confidence. He was a winner and he knew it. So... [You guessed it] he kept on eating and eating and eating, and he ate and he ate and he ate.

However, the other contestant, Claude-Jean Papillon from one of the most well-stocked closets of Paree also just kept on eating and eating... [and so on]. And you know what? Willie couldn't keep up. No matter how hard he tried, he just couldn't keep up.

He tried to continue eating...and...e-a-t-i-n-g...and eat... And he couldn't force down even one more bite. He pushed back his chair, stumbled from the table, jumped off the platform, and ran to his mama.

Of course, she tried to tell him that it was OK. There'd be another contest the next year. And maybe he'd win then. But tears were running out of poor little Willie's eyes. And he just couldn't stop crying. He kept on crying and crying and crying And he cried and he cried and he cried. And: DID YOU EVER SEE A MOTH BAWL?!

Storytellers often present programs at playgrounds as part of the summer actvities sponsored by city departments of parks and recreation. At these events, the tellers present a continuing series of stoires, just as they frequently do in schools and libraries.

Stories often are told at county fairs, festivals, craft fairs and, quite logically, at book fairs. If you're interested, you might investigate these. One good way to go about it is to see if there's a storyteller's organization in your area. Many cities have them; their members have monthly meetings where they tell stories. They go to and often participate in other storytelling events. They tell stories at cafes, schools, storytelling conventions, and so on.

Many of these groups, such as the one in San Diego, present storytelling "concerts" at colleges and universities, where either one teller or a number of tellers present an entire evening's entertainment.

There are many people from all areas of the country who make a large part of their living from telling stories. You can read about them in books such as *Homespun Tales from America's Favorite Storytellers.* Jimmy Neil Smith, the author, is founder and director of the National Association for the Preservation and Perpetuation of Storytelling.

AUDIENCE AND PLACE

No matter what the situation, you should figure out as much about your audience as you can, not only so you know what to expect from them but also so that you can choose a fitting story to tell.

You need to consider the reason for the audience's meeting. Is it to be entertained? Is it to celebrate a holiday or someone's retirement? Is it to learn something? If so, is the meeting voluntary or compulsory? You need to know this in order to determine how much extra work, if any, you'll need to do to win the audience over to the idea of listening to you.

What are the particular interests of the group, and how can you relate your telling to these interests? For example, how might you approach a historical society as opposed to a meeting of business women? The point is there should be few surprises when you appear in front of a group, especially if you have found out as much as you can about the event and the occasion.

Part of this involves knowing the location and checking it out ahead of time, if possible. Will it be in a restaurant where waiters are running in and out and dishes are clattering? Will it be in an outdoor mall, where you have the distraction of people wandering in and out of the telling area?

If you need any special equipment, such as a chalkboard or a record player, is there room for it? Should you bring your own, or will it be supplied?

Obviously, you should be positioned so there is no strong light behind you, or your listeners may have to squint. Neither should there be movement behind you. If possible, position yourself in front of a wall or cutain. It's also distracting to both you and the listeners when you appear in an open space where people constantly cross through the telling area.

Most important, make sure, if you can, that you will be in a location where you can be easily seen and heard. More than any other performing or living art, storytelling involves an intimacy between teller and audience. Podiums, proscenium arches, and platforms all can interfere with this intimacy. Theatre often deliberately provides barriers in the imaginary fourth wall between actor and audience member. This should not be the case in a storytelling situation.

At times, of course, an audience will be too large for one-on-one eye contact. In these circumstances, do your best—by using intimate tone and looking to all parts of the audience—to convey to each listener that you are speaking directly to him and her. Sometimes having a telling circle, which many storytellers prefer, isn't possible and you end up somewhat separated. Even though the separation is physical, try to diminish or eliminate the psychological barriers.

Exercises

1. Choose a situation, either real or imaginary, for telling a story, e.g., a religious service, a holiday, a community gathering. Now, keeping this situation in mind, try to discover a story to tell to the following specific audiences: a) children five years old and younger; b) children six to nine; c) children ten to thirteen; d) young adults; and e) adults.

2. Attend a storytelling event or a speech in which you think one or more stories will be told. (Maybe you can find some listed in your newspaper.) Pay attention to the teller's technique, and figure out what you like and dislike about it.

3. Determine a place and situation where you would be able to tell a story. Analyze the location and the type of audience, and choose a story to tell there. If possible, actually tell it.

4. Develop a story from your own personal experience: either a story with a moral, a nostalgia piece, or a humorous tale.

5. Take one of the stories from this chapter and tell it to an audience at a telling event, to a family gathering, to one or two members of your family, or to one or more friends. Remember that the best stories often are told in informal settings.

3. SELECTING A STORY TO TELL

The best story for you to tell may not be the best one for others to tell. The story has to suit you and your personality. If you are a quiet person, you probably won't want to tell an extremely bombastic story. And vice versa. If you are very much an extrovert, you may feel confined if you are unable to use a lot of movement and changes in voice.

PREREQUISITES FOR CHOOSING A STORY

Do You Like It?

First of all, when looking for a story to tell, choose one that you not only think you can tell comfortably, but one you like. You'll be spending a lot of time reading, learning, and analyzing the story before you ever present it, so you'll want one you are pretty certain you won't get tired of. And, if you're really interested in storytelling, you'll want to build a repertoire. That is, you'll want to have many stories to tell, all of which can be told time and time again. So you'll want each story to continue to hold your interest. If you end up with a story that bores you, more than likely it will bore an audience because your heart won't be in telling it.

Do You Agree with It?

Be certain you agree with the content of the story. If it goes against your beliefs, you probably shouldn't consider telling it.

Even when building a repertoire of stories for all occasions, you'll want to consider the type of audience to whom you'll most likely tell stories. Then choose stories accordingly. If you are going to be telling to very young children, you'll probably want to stay away from tall tales, for instance, because young kids may not have the experience or knowledge to appreciate them. On the other hand, if you'll be telling mostly to teenagers or adults, you probably won't want to include many nonsense tales.

What Is Your Purpose?

In addition to the audience's age, consider the purpose you'll have most often in telling stories. Will the stories be part of religious education? Will they be part of longer talks? Will their purpose be to interest children in literature, to entertain, to acquaint audiences with past times? Whatever the reason, you have to be able to find or develop stories that fit.

For example, you would probably not tell "Willie the Moth" as part of a longer talk because it takes so much time to tell. (For me, it usually took about twenty minutes.) Nor would you be likely to tell fairy tales to teenagers, who like to think of themselves as more sophisticated than to be interested in them.

Will the Story Mean Something to Your Audience?

Unless it's just for entertainment, a story should mean something. It should help the listeners in some way to appreciate life, to understand a particular facet of living, to rejoice in life's richness. That is, it has to deal with something relevant to the lives of the listeners.

Is the Story Tellable?

But most important, a story has to be tellable. There are many written pieces that would not translate especially well to oral presentation. They're too complex, too descriptive, too lengthy, and so on.

You need to choose a story with a simple action or plot line, without unnecessary forays into secondary plots or loosely related episodes. That sort of thing is fine for a novel or even a written short story, but would only confuse listeners who, unlike readers, cannot go back and look up something they missed.

In other words, the story should have **unity**; everything should relate to one central action or set of circumstances. It should deal with one protagonist or central character, and everything that happens should relate to that character. If it's a story with a plot, then all the action must somehow have bearing on whether or not the protagonist wins by reaching a particular goal, which should be apparent from the beginning.

For example, Willie the Moth's goal is to win all the contests and be the world champion. Nothing deviates from that action. On the other hand, "Threshing Day" has no plot, as such. It's a reminiscence or personal experience piece. Still, the listener should realize right from the beginning that everything in it relates to the central idea: threshing day. There is nothing at all extraneous about the piece.

Part of choosing a story to tell, then, is recognizing what is acceptable story form and what an audience, through accepting the contract of listener, has a right to expect.

Who are the Characters?

Another important consideration is characterization. Do the protagonist and antagonist come across as real? How about the secondary characters? Are there too many characters, which might confuse the listener? What about the character's names? Are they easy to remember? Are they dissimilar enough so that they won't be confused? If there are more than two or three names, they should not be of similar length or even have the same beginning letters, such as Ben, Bob, and Bill do. If the names are

47

unfamiliar, make sure they are easy to remember. If, for example, the story is populated by too many Russian-sounding or Chinese-sounding names, and your audience is not of Russian or Chinese background, most likely they'll get lost in who is which character.

Is the Language Appropriate?

Make sure the story you choose has appropriate language. This means several things. Is it appropriate to the age group, either not too complicated or too simple? Are the sentences easy to follow, rather than being long and convoluted? Does the story use informal rather than formal language? Part of this, of course, depends on your adaptation of the story, which will be discussed in the next chapter.

The story should not have a lot of tongue twisters or difficult pronunciations, unless its purpose is to provide humor by using them.

Will the Story Have a Positive Influence?

Any experience we have changes us in some way, whether minutely or to a great extent. Decide if you think the story you choose will change the listeners in a positive way. Will they be somehow better—happier, more knowledgeable on something important, etc.—by what you tell them? In other words, does the story have something worthwhile to say, and does it convey this in an effective manner? Does it give you joy to tell it, as well as bring joy to the listener? If any of these questions are answered in the negative, it probably is better to choose another story.

How Much Description and Dialogue?

Good description often gives added beauty to written language. However, it slows down the action in a storytelling situation. Certainly, you need some description so the listeners can understand what the characters and the setting are like, but don't choose a story that has long descriptive passages.

Avoid stories that are mostly dialogue. If you don't, you risk confusing the audience. When reading a story, it's difficult enough to keep track of who is speaking, but if readers do get lost, they can go back and figure things out. Listeners have no such advantage. Certainly, in using dialogue, you may want to vary voice usage for each change, and this helps. But overall, too much dialogue, like too much description, makes the listener impatient to get on with the story.

Does the Story Have Rhythm?

Often, told stories have a lot of repetition and a particular rhythm. Young children especially like this sort of thing, as can be seen in the popularity of nursery rhymes and jump rope chants, which can reassure a child by presenting the expected or familiar.

As I indicated with "Willie," both repetition and rhythm can be enhanced by audience participation, which is important whenever practical because it insures that the audience actually wants to pay attention to the story. Any time we are actively involved in something, there's a better chance we will stay with and enjoy it.

The following White Mountain Apache story uses many of the other devices mentioned above.

THE WINNING OF DAWN
told by Charlie Sago

Long ago it was dark all the time. Then all animals talked and acted like people. The animals were divided into two bands. In one band were all those animals that crawled and had poison, like snakes, bugs, or lizards. Bear was chief of this band. In the other band were the good animals, and their chief was Slim Coyote. They had no stars, moon, or sun then, but Slim Coyote's band wanted these and daylight. Bear and his band wanted it to stay as it was, dark all the time. Slim Coyote and his people decided to play Bear and his band a game of hidden ball, to decide which group should have their way about the daylight. The two bands arranged to play the game. If Bear's people won, it was to stay dark, and they would kill Slim Coyote and all his band. If Slim Coyote's followers won, it was to become daylight and they were to have sun, moon, and stars as they are today. They would have the right also to kill Bear and all his band.

The game was started, Bear's people sitting with him on one side of the big fire, and Slim Coyote's band on the other side. One of Slim Coyote's band, yayi'i'i, was very good at the game. As they played, Coyote would sing, "Dawn, dawn, let it dawn," and it would start to grow light in the east, like dawn. Then Bear's turn would come, and he would sing, "No dawn, no dawn," and it would get dark again. This way they went on. Coyote started to win. When Bear sang, it didn't get dark anymore. When Coyote sang the world got lighter all the time. The game was getting close now, and each band put guards out around the gamblers to keep them from leaving. If anyone went out to urinate, they were made to come right back. Pretty soon Bear said, "I am going to my camp to get my tobacco pouch before we finish the game." "No," Slim Coyote's people said, "you must stay here till the game is finished." Bear said, "You will kill us all anyway, as you have almost won the game. Let me go and I will come right back," so they let him go. When Bear got to his camp, he put his moccasins on wrong, right for left, and left for right; then ran away. As soon as Bear left, Slim Coyote's band started killing Bear's people. They killed all but a few. Yellow Rattlesnake hid himself in the sand, close to the fire, and so was saved. Black Rattlesnake crawled into a crack in the rocks and tried to hide, but they found him and shot him where he lay with arrows. All this happened far to the north, and to this day you can see the arrows sticking in the crack of rock where Black Rattlesnake was killed. Bear ran off into a swampy place, because they were after him. There he hid in the mud and was not found. Because of the way Bear acted at that time is why he is still so mean and ugly today. From that time on the sun rose and set, and they had daylight and moon and stars at night.

Will It Hold an Audience's Attention?

To hold an audience's attention, a story needs to have suspense. This means the audience will want to know whether or not the central character will reach the goal, or, if it's not a story with a plot, simply how it will be concluded.

Usually, when we think of action in a story, we think of advancement toward a plot. But this need not be the case. There are many stories, particularly from the oral tradition, that do not start with an inciting incident and continue to build to a climax, as a story with a plot does. Instead, they may hold our attention in that they are concerned with something unusual or different. Or, on the other hand, they may be about something familiar, which we enjoy hearing discussed.

Certainly, we've all heard the Christmas story from the Bible many times. Yet its familiarity and its meaning continue to hold our attention. It contains the action and suspense of Mary and Joseph seeking a place to spend the night, of the wise men traveling to see the Baby Jesus, and of Herod's decree that all the male babies are to be killed. A story such as this inspires wonder in us, which is another consideration in choosing something to tell.

What Is the Story's Theme?

Generally, too, a story should have only one theme, which should be clear and simple. It should answer such questions as: Does love really always triumph? Will good actions truly be rewarded?

Most of the time a theme has to do with a common belief or common premise, such as the two above. We can usually state the theme of a story in terms of an adage—a wise, old saying. People who live in glass houses shouldn't throw stones. The love of money is the root of all evil. A stitch in time saves nine, and so on.

What do you think is the theme of the following?

THE GUILTY WOMAN

This is the story of a man who was very rich. He had so much cattle that he could barter them for more wives than any other man—if the chief is not counted. No, he was a very wealthy man.

One day he went to hunt, but he was very unlucky. He brought no game back to his village. All that he could find was a tortoise. He took it to his first wife and asked her to cook it for him, for the hunger had caught him.

But that big wife said: "*H-ha!* I do not cook such things as tortoises! Give that sort of work to one of your other wives!"

Then he went to the second one, and she also said, "*H-ha!*", for she did not cook tortoises. Then he went to the third one, the fourth one, and all the other others, but they all said, "*H-ha!*", for they would not cook such a thing as a tortoise.

But the youngest one, she who was the littlest one, said, "No, that will be good, Father. I shall cook it for you."

Then she cooked the tortoise. She cooked it, she cooked it, and when it was tender and done, she dished it up in a little clay bowl, together with the gravy, and she covered it with a little grass mat so that the dogs and cats could not get at it. And, after she had put it on a low wall outside the hut, she went to the veld to gather broom grass.

That afternoon, when she came home, the husband was sitting by the fire, and he asked, "Little wife, where were you for such a long time? I told you I was very hungry. Bring me meat so that I can eat."

"Here it is, Big Man," said she, and gave him the dish with the little grass mat over it. He took it. *Yoalo. Yoalo. Yoalo.*

He laughed when he took it, and he smacked his lips. But when he looked inside, he saw that there was no meat in that dish, and no gravy either. Everything had been eaten up. Only the shell of the tortoise lay in the dish.

Yo, he was cross with that wife!

"You have eaten it!" he shouted at her, for the skin on his stomach was black with hunger.

"It is not I who ate it, Grandfather," she said. "It is the truth that I speak. I did not eat it. Not at all. It is also not a dog or a cat that ate it, for I put it in a safe place, and it was well covered with the little grass mat, as you saw for yourself."

But the hunger and the yearning for the meat made him quite crazy. He did not want to believe her. He said: "I am going to the witch doctor right now. His magic bones will speak and tell me whether it was you who ate my meat. Then I shall know."

Then he went. He went, and when he came there he and the owner of those magic bones talked for a long while about the payment. They talked, talked, talked until the magic bones and the magic stones were satisfied with the price. Then they told the witch doctor that they were willing to tell the stranger what he wanted to know.

Then the witch doctor once more scattered the bones and the stones in front of him on the ground, and they spoke to him as tea leaves speak to some people.

Everything that the stones and the bones said, their master repeated word for word to the man. They could not tell him who had taken the meat, but they gave him a good plan to find out who it had been.

He went home and did as those magic bones and stones had told him to do.

He took a long thong that had been plaited from the sinews of a kudu. He took it to the deep pool in the river, and he took all the people of his village with him, the men and the women and the children. His own wives and their children also. That was what the bones had told him to do.

When they reached the pool, he gave that rope of sinews to the two strongest men and said: "One must stand on this side and hold one end of the rope. The other must take the other end and go and stand on the other side of the pool."

That was what the magic bones of the clever man had said. And the two men did just so. *Yoalo. Yoalo. Yoalo.*

They spanned a bridge over the pool with that rope of sinews, and, when they had done so, the man called his little wife, she who had cooked the tortoise. He commanded her:

"You go and walk over the water on that rope. From this side to that side. If the kudu's sinews snap and you fall in the water, all the people here will know it was you who ate the meat that was meant for me, and drank the gravy that was meant for me. If the rope does not break, everybody will know that you are innocent."

The little wife did as the man had commanded her. She trod on the rope; she trod, she trod, and then she walked. Very carefully. Below her the water went *shoo-shoo, shoo-shoo,* but she walked. She walked, and as she walked she sang:

> Sinews of kudu, break...that I might fall,
> That in the water I might fall...that I might fall,
> They say I ate the tortoise...that I might fall,
> But tortoise I did not eat...that I might fall...

She walked. She sang. She walked. She sang. She walked, but the sinews did not break; they carried her to the other side of the dark pool of water in safety.

Then everybody knew that she was innocent. It was not she who had eaten the tortoise meat.

Now another wife had to walk over the water, on the thin rope plaited of kudu sinews. When this wife walked, she sang the same song that the little one had sung:

> Sinews of kudu, break...that I might fall,
> That in the water I might fall...that I might fall,
> *Yoalo, yoalo, yoalo...*

But the sinews did not break. They did not break at all, but carried her safely to the other side of the water. And everybody saw that she was innocent. *Hm,* it was a strange business!

And so the man called all his wives who sat there waiting for their turn to walk over the water on that rope. And everyone who walked sang the same song:

> Sinews of kudu, break...that I might fall,
> *Yoalo,* that I might fall, *yoalo, yoalo,*
> Sinews of kudu, break...that I might fall...

But the sinews did not break. They stayed whole and carried every wife, one after the other, to safety. *Yoalo. Yoalo.*

55

But then they came to the last one, the big wife who had been the first to refuse to cook the tortoise for their husband.

"Now it is your turn, Mother," he said to her.

Then she stood up and trod on the rope, as the others had done. One foot in front of the other. Cautiously, cautiously. And as she walked, she sang the song that all the others had sung:

> Sinews of kudu, break...that I might fall,
> That in the water I might fall...that I might fall,
> They say I ate the tortoise...that I might fall,
> But the tortoise I did not eat...that I might fall...
> Just so. *Yoalo.*

She walked, one foot in front of the other. One foot in front of the other, but when she came to the middle of that deep, dark pool, the rope broke. It broke and *twaaah!* the big wife fell into the water. Before everybody's eyes she disappeared in the depths of that water.

Then everybody knew it was she who had eaten the meat of the tortoise and had drunk the gravy. And they saw how she was punished by drowning.

No, it is right so, said everybody as they walked home. The old people say that you must stoop when you come to your own possessions, but when you come to those of others you must stand up straight. Which means that you must keep your hands off that which belongs to other people.

Now, that big wife had stooped when she came to her husband's food, and she took it, and she ate it. But the magic bones had made a good plan. So they had spoken, and so it had happened. No, it was right so.

And this is the end of the story.

The preceding story fits the oral tradition very well. It has a brief opening, which establishes the problem: the fact that the hunter has been unsuccessful in finding any meat except for that of a tortoise, and he's hungry. Immediately the scene is set, characters are simply introduced and the story plunges into the action line. All these are important in gaining and holding the attention of the listener.

Is Your Story Faithful to the Original?

Another consideration in choosing a story concerns whether the version you find is faithful to the source, even though the language is changed. Obviously, the African story has been translated into English, but we can probably assume that it is true to the original version because we can tell it evokes visions of a culture different than ours and presents it vividly.

"The Guilty Woman," of course, also has dramatic appeal. We stay with it because we want to know the outcome. This should be the case with all stories we hear or tell.

FINDING STORIES

Finding a story you want to tell often takes or can take more time than preparing and learning it because you need to take time to "live" with a potential story.

Five Sources

There are five general sources for finding a story: libraries and collections; books on storytelling; other storytellers; jokes and anecdotes, which you expand; and your own experiences.

Libraries and Collections

The two stories in this chapter came from collections I found in a university library. Similarly, the city library has many collections. They're grouped under such categories as ethnic stories;

myths and folktales; fairy tales; Bible stories; stories for holidays, and so on. If the collections indicate that these are traditional stories, that they are not copyrighted under a single author's name, then you can feel free to use them and adapt them to your own particular needs.

You need to keep searching for good stories by being alert to what you hear and by browsing in bookstores and libraries. If you find something you like, keep going over it. If you continue to like it, it's a pretty good indication that it's something you would like to tell and can be successful in telling.

Books on Storytelling

In books on storytelling, such as those listed in the bibliography of this book, you'll usually find collections of stories as well as individual stories—sometimes traditional tales, sometimes those developed by the teller. Generally, these books, written specifically for storytellers, have a larger variety of stories than you will find in most other collections.

Other Storytellers

Similarly, you may hear stories told that you yourself would like to tell. It's a good idea, however, to ask the teller's permission to use the story. Maybe the teller will be reluctant to grant permission unless you intend to change the story to fit your own personality.

Jimmy Neil Smith, in *Homespun Tales from America's Favorite Storytellers*, includes an anecdote about a man approaching storyteller Laura Simms and asking if she had told a certain story. She said she didn't recognize it and asked him to tell her more about it. When he did, she realized that, yes, it had started out as her story. But the man had seen it so differently that he developed an entirely new version, not even realizing it.

Jokes

Often you can take a simple joke and expand it into a story, building and elaborating on it. Years ago I heard a joke about a man who'd had a very hard life but always managed to keep going because "he was rough and tough and hard to bluff and used to hardships." The punch line relied on verbal wit in that the guy finally was able to find a job working on a ship. He was told to go up to the crow's nest to look out over the ocean for other ships. When he'd nearly reached his destination, he slipped and fell, from a height of sixty feet or so down to the deck. Everyone on board was horrified; they felt certain the man was dead, every bone in his body broken. Not so. He stood up, brushed himself off and laughed. You see, he was rough and tough and used to *hard ships.*

I took the story, very snort in its original form, and changed it into a saga of this man's life, almost from the time of birth up until he obtains his job. The telling easily took twenty or twenty-five minutes, with the hero going from misfortune to misfortune.

Real Life

You also can take incidents from your life, whether serious or funny, and present them more or less the way they actually happened, or expand upon them. Remember, stories don't have to be the literal truth if they present a larger truth. You also don't necessarily need to use your own life as the basis. You can take other people's lives or even historical events you've read about, personalize them, and present them as stories. In the next chapter is a story, "Millennium," in which I did just that.

Don't be afraid to be personal when preparing a story. Often we like particular stories because they do relate to something close to us. If we have emotional wounds that have never healed, it often helps to exorcise them by telling about them in a story.

I based the following on something similar that happened to me as a teenager, which affected me for years. It had a cathartic effect for me to "get it out of my system" in this way. This is only an excerpt from a longer piece, but it presents the central problem. To set the scene, Martin is seventeen and has been told by his father to stop disagreeing with his grandfather. He doesn't listen, but keeps on arguing.

Martin's father, Dan, grabbed his arm and yanked him through the kitchen and into the living room. He was a powerful man. A good three inches shorter than Martin, still he outweighed him.

Martin tried to struggle free, but Dan's grip tightened. He slammed Martin into a corner, grabbed him around the neck and began to squeeze. At the same time he pounded Martin's head into the corner of the wall.

Stop, Martin thought, please stop! Dan had hurt him before but never this bad. Martin's vision began to go, first at the periphery, like someone's shutting a gate across his eyes. He grabbed Dan's wrists and tried to pry the hands from around his neck. Dan squeezed harder.

Suddenly, his mother ran down the steps and into the living room. "Dan!" she screamed. "What are you doing?" She ran toward him and grabbed his arm. "Stop, for God's sake, stop! You're going to kill him."

Dan released him and stepped back. Martin staggered forward, then caught his balance. There was a ring of fire around his neck.

He ran to the kitchen and grabbed his coat from a hook by the door. He shrugged into it and stumbled outside and down the steps of the porch.

It was clear and cold. He ran down Second Street and turned up the hill. By the time he got to Sixth a headache was making him ill. He slowed to a walk. He knew Dan was frustrated; money was scarce. Most of the kids he taught had quit because they couldn't pay for lessons. But Martin couldn't help that. His dad didn't need to take it out on him.

His feet crunched the grass at the side of the road, breaking the blades like thin glass. It was a beautiful night; the stars shone brightly. The sky was a solid blue. He headed down the highway toward Clivesville. The jacket rubbed his neck. He unzipped it and took it off. So what if he got sick? The wind blew through his shirt, like icy water down his back. Where was he going anyhow? What was he going to do? Nobody cared; he wasn't sure he cared himself. His father treated him like he was worthless, so maybe he was.

Maybe he'd freeze to death, and that would be the end. Maybe he'd try to help things along. He fluffed his jacket into a pillow and laid it on the white center line of the macadam road. He lay down, his head in the middle of his jacket, and drew his legs up to his chest, then closed his eyes to wait. If he were lucky, it would all end quickly.

The night was still. Occasionally, a leaf blew by or he heard a far-off car horn.

He began to shiver and couldn't control his body. The running and the walking had made him sweat, and the sweat was beginning to freeze.

Time passed as in a dream. Finally, he sat up and drew his arms around his knees. The trees made stark silhouettes against the light of the moon. Stars twinkled hundreds of light years away. Some might even be dead now, he thought, their light still beaming to earth.

Martin stood and put on his jacket. Would he have let a car run over him? He didn't know, but he didn't think so. He didn't want to die, did he? Sometimes he had trouble deciding what was real and what was only his imagination.

He wondered what he should do. For the time being, he decided, he'd keep on walking. In another four or five miles he'd be in Clivesville.

Collecting stories and telling them take a lot of patience. You cannot simply decide one day to be a storyteller and have it be an accomplished fact the next. You need to read a lot and listen to other storytellers. You have to really pay attention to stories, and then let them grow in your imagination.

Exercises

1. Find a story that you like and then try to analyze why you like it. Why did it appeal to you?

2. Find a story in a collection. Read over it several times to see if you still like it and want to tell it. How might you want to change it?

3. Find a story to tell in which you can use audience participation.

4. With a particular type of audience in mind, find a story that you think you might like to tell. Why would it appeal to that audience?

5. Take a joke that you have heard or read, and expand it into a story for a particular audience.

6. Take a personal experience, either painful or joyful, and use it as the basis of a story you develop for a particular audience.

4. ADAPTING YOUR STORY

In preceding chapters the need to adapt a story has been mentioned several times. What does this mean? Exactly what should you do when adapting a story to fit your telling?

Obviously, you should adapt the story into something with which you'd be comfortable. That means if you're uncomfortable with any of the vocabulary, you can change it. It means that if any sections of the story in any way offend you, you can try to alter them.

Of course, then, there's the question of dialect. For the most part, dialect is all right if you feel comfortable with it and if you have the ability to use it. It is not all right if it offends any particular ethnic group. For instance, I immediately eliminated from consideration for this book any stories I thought unflattering. In some cases, the stories themselves were acceptable, but the misuse of grammar and the mispronunciation of words was not because it implied certain people were unintelligent.

WHAT STORIES ARE OK TO CHANGE?

Any stories that come from the oral tradition can be changed to fit the teller. They are not copyrighted. You should, of course, try to be true to the spirit and meaning of these stories. If you don't agree with what they say overall and how they say it, you probably shouldn't consider using them.

You can get into trouble when you take well-known stories and try to change them. It would be plain silly, for instance, to change the wolf to a bear in "Little Red Riding Hood," even though a bear is larger and could more logically devour a human being.

Stories that are authored should not be changed. The writer put them down in a certain way because he/she felt that way was most effective. Even if authored stories are no longer protected by copyright, the teller has a moral obligation not to change them.

The following story already has undergone many changes in that it appears in many different countries, in many different versions, going back hundreds of years. Here it is a Mexican tale. Would you change it if you planned to tell it? Why or why not? In what way would you consider changing it?

REPAYING GOOD WITH EVIL

This was a wise man who, while walking along the trail, found a serpent in a trap.

"Let me out," begged the serpent. "It's wrong to keep me here."

"You are right," said the wise man. "It is wrong to keep one trapped." Thereupon he released the snake.

Immediately the serpent coiled about his benefactor and prepared to eat him.

"This is not right," said the wise man. "It is wrong to repay good with evil."

"Perhaps," replied the serpent, "but I am hungry."

"That I regret," said the wise man. "It is wrong to repay good with evil. Before you devour me, let's ask the opinion of someone else."

"That would only prolong your worry, for he would agree with me," said the serpent. "However, to please you, we will call a judge."

They spied a horse passing near. "Come here," called the wise man. "Come here, Senor Caballo. We want your opinion in a serious dispute."

The horse approached and heard impartially the pleas of each. "It is indeed not right for one to repay good with evil," said he. Then, fearing the wrath of the serpent, he added, "But on the other hand, *es la costumbre* (it is the custom) that good be repaid with evil. Behold myself, for example. Once I was young, had the best of food, and was happy, and it was with my energy that my master became a rich man. Now that I am old, he has turned me out to starve. Yes, *es la costumbre* to repay good with evil."

Then the serpent called the ox. "Brother Ox," said the serpent, "we have called you to hear our cause and give an opinion. My friend here contends that it is wrong to repay good with evil. What is your judgment?"

The ox looked the facts calmly in the face and meditated and chewed his cud. Then, with a tired sigh, he said, "Whether it is right or wrong is not the case. *Es la costumbre* to repay good with evil."

"Fine," said the serpent to the wise man. "Now I shall devour you."

"We are but little wiser than we were," pleaded the wise man. "Grant that we hear the opinion of one more judge."

Thereupon they called the coyote. "'Mano Coyote," said the wise man, "my friend the serpent contends that it is right to repay good with evil. *Que dices?*"

"I had rather not say without due thought. I am just *gente corriente* (common folks), a wild animal from the chaparral. My judgment at best may be of little use. What is the trouble?"

The story was told how the snake was released by the wise man and then how the former was wanting to devour the latter when the wise man said that it was not right to repay good with evil.

"That is not good enough," said 'Mano Coyote. "I desire to study the case more in detail. Now just how was the serpent trapped? Show me where and show me the trap and show me just how he was fastened, for it might be that he was never trapped at all."

The serpent feared the suggestion that the trap was only a trick. He placed himself as the wise man had found him.

"Now is that really the way you were fastened in, Mr. Snake?" asked the coyote.

"It is," said the snake.

"Is that really the way he was caught?" he asked the wise man.

"It is," said the wise man.

"Then it is my judgment that the situation as it stands is better than it was when I found it. That is all."

"But it isn't right to leave him to die," said the wise man.

"If it isn't," said the coyote, "it's his own affair."

The wise man and the coyote walked away.

When out of hearing, the coyote said to the wise man, "Brother Wise Man, you will not deny that I have saved your life."

"No," said the wise man. "Though your decision was not definite, at least you saved my life. Look! I own a ranch near here. Come there at eight every morning from now on after I have tied up the dog and I shall give you a hen."

"Good!" said the coyote. "That is better; that is repaying good with good."

The coyote found life so easy he became lazy and took to strong drink, insisting that his appetite was bad and that he needed a *traguito* each morning before eating a hen. Then within a few days he complained that the *traguito* of *sotol* increased his appetite so much that one hen would not do. The wise man was compelled to add a bottle of *sotol* and another hen to the menu.

"It seems," meditated the wise man, "that after all, good is repaid with evil. It was right to give the coyote something but now my friend is resorting to blackmail."

"And that isn't all," growled the dog. "Ere long, he will call for another hen. I know him; he lives by his wits."

"That would be my ruin," said the wise man. "What should one do?"

"Put him off one day," said the dog, "then put me in the sack with the hens and when he calls for another chicken, let me out. I will attend to him."

Before long, the coyote began to hint that one bottle of *sotol* and two hens were poor pay for the saving of a life. "It seems you have forgotten that good must be repaid with good," said he to the wise man.

"It seems, 'Mano Coyote," answered the latter, "that you have forgotten that at one time you said one hen a day was enough."

"But time changes all. The first contract is now unsatisfactory," answered the coyote. "It is my desire now that I be paid three bottles of *sotol* and three hens daily."

"Very well," said the wise man, "tomorrow I shall begin the new arrangements."

The following morning at the appointed time the wise man came to the meeting place with three bottles of *sotol* and three sacks.

"*Ay, carray!* Toss me out a hen."

The wise man did. The coyote devoured her, feathers and all, and then drank another bottle of *sotol*.

"*Ay, que carray,*" he shouted. "Toss me out another hen."

The wise man released another hen. The coyote pounced upon her and ate her quicker than the first.

"*Carramba!*" he said. "With age and experience my appetite grows. Now give me the other bottle of *sotol.*"

After finishing the third bottle, he shouted, "Let her out."

The wise man released the dog from the sack. The poor coyote was too drunk and stuffed to run. He was caught, but before the fangs of the dog had found their mark the coyote called to the wise man, "It isn't right to repay good with evil. Call off your dog."

"Perhaps it isn't right," answered the wise man, "but *es la costumbre.*"

SPECIFIC CHANGES

Change the Point of View

To make a story more specifically yours, you may want to change the point of view. This might mean changing third person to first person, as though the events happened to the narrator of the tale rather than to another person. For example, you might change the above story:

O nce when I was walking along the trail from my house, I found a serpent in a trap.

"Let me out," begged the serpent. "It's wrong to keep me here."

"You are right," I said. "It is wrong to keep one trapped." Thereupon I released him.

You might want to change the viewpoint from male to female and vice versa. In the story at the end of this chapter, if you are a man, you might want to tell the story from the viewpoint of someone observing the woman. For instance:

I never understood why Vida, my sister, ever married Jerome Maugham. From the beginning it was a failure for never could she reach him. And as she often told me, Maugham refused to discuss the situation.

As you'll see, if you compare the two opening versions of "Millennium," I tried to keep the tone of the piece true to the style in which it was written. Otherwise, I might have said something like:

I don't know why Vida, my sister, and Jerome Maugham ever got married. She told me a lot of times that right from the beginning she knew it was a failure.

This second rewrite suggests a more contemporary flavor and not only ruins the original flavor, but is inconsistent with the time, which, as the title indicates, is 1000 A.D.

Mostly, of course, it's a matter of using common sense. For some reason, women are more able to get away with being male narrators in stories they tell than vice versa. If you were a man, you'd have to be a very skillful teller to get away with assuming a woman's point of view throughout.

A second way a man might tell "Millennium" is from a third person point of view:

Vida's marriage to Jerome Maugham admittedly was a failure. Never could she reach him. She thought that perhaps he would say the same of her. She didn't know.

Change the Time Period

Another change you might want to make is to change the historical period. Maybe you feel that you can make it more applicable or at least more acceptable to your listener by having a contemporary setting.

The language in "Repaying Good with Evil" is fairly contemporary, though there are no slang terms. Still, the story has been traced back to at least the twelfth century, and certainly has been changed as it's been handed down. In many cases, this is what preserves a story. Sometimes, not only is the language updated, but so are the circumstances. But this is not always the case. Many fables, for instance, survive without this sort of updating.

Rearrange the Plot

A different kind of change you might consider is rearranging the plot. You may want to do this to create more suspense or to place more emphasis on one point than on another. Again, this is acceptable if you don't totally change the original intention, unless you are doing it for fun and the audience is in on it.

James Thurber, for example, in *A Thurber Carnival,* took many well-known fairy tales and fables and changed them around to make them funny.

You also may want to change narration into dialogue, keeping in mind, of course, that too much dialogue can be confusing. This can make the story more interesting in that the narrator can change the voice for changes in character.

Add or Delete Characters

You may want either to add or delete characters. In "Willie the Moth," I added a lot of characters, such as Uncle Randolph and Mama, who were not there in the original version. Or you may want to cut out characters who you feel are unnecessary or add little to the story. In the African story from the last chapter, you might either expand the role of the wives and give them dialogue or cut some of them out.

Lengthen or Shorten the Story

One of the nice things about storytelling is that you can make a story either long or short, depending both on the circumstances and on the response from the audience. In other words, you can compress it by cutting out characters and detail and by simplifying the plot. Or you can build it up as I did with the joke about hardships.

DEVELOPING YOUR OWN STORY

Each teller, of course, is an individual. Each develops a unique method of presenting a story or a program of stories. That's good; we wouldn't want to be clones of one another. Individuality can hold attention and provide interest. Just be sure you develop the best method of telling that you can. But keep in mind that what is best for you probably won't be for anyone else, and vice versa.

Personal Experience

Both "Threshing Day" and the excerpt from the story about the boy being strangled come from personal experience, which begins to show that you can take almost any type of experience and make it into a story. You can start with the facts and go on from there. The only guidelines are that it's interesting and that you feel comfortable with it.

Many storytellers develop most of their material from their own backgrounds or from family members' and friends' experiences. For example, I could make stories out of such things as the time my paternal grandfather hid the money in the stove. Or the time my maternal grandfather nearly drowned when his own father threw him in a dam to teach him to swim. Or, going another direction entirely, about the time a friend of mine was abducted as a little girl in London and driven around for hours before being let out of the car; and how now, as a result of this, she becomes completely lost each time she's more than two blocks from home.

It doesn't matter whether you tell stories that already are in existence or those that you develop yourself. What does matter is the effect on the audience and whether you accomplish whatever your purpose is in telling them.

Toys or Nursery Rhymes

Besides using people's experiences to tell stories, you can simply invent things about particular toys, or change and expand

73

nursery rhymes into long tales. You can even tell total nonsense as a kind of vocal rhythm.

AUDIENCE PARTICIPATION

As mentioned earlier, you may want to develop stories that require audience participation. Besides repetitious phrases, as in "Willie the Moth," you may want to assign sound effects, such as the wind blowing. A popular story at camps and playgrounds is "Jungle Safari," in which the teller asks the audience members to do such things as rub their palms together to simulate going through high grass or slap palms on thighs to indicate walking on solid ground.

You may even want to assign particular roles to audience members in which each person has a phrase to repeat each time you so indicate.

You may want to tell stories that involve objects, such as a chalkboard or flannel board. You may use puppets, or enhance your story with the use of slides or cutouts. It doesn't matter. Whatever adds rather than detracts from the telling is a good device.

Exercises

1. Investigate stories that use dialect. Try out some of the dialects to see if you're comfortable with them. If so, practice a story using a dialect. If not, change the story so the dialect becomes unnecessary.

2. Find several stories you like but you think need adaptations. Try adapting them in several ways—by expanding or compressing, by changing the point of view, by adding or deleting characters, by cutting out or adding dialogue, and so on. Don't outlaw the use of a story simply because it doesn't at first seem to fit your personality.

3. Take a well-known fable or fairy tale and change it to make it funny. Maybe you can investigate writers such as Thurber to see what they've done.

4. Develop a story using some sort of props.

5. Develop a story where you assign different roles (animate or not) to members of the audience.

6. Adapt the story on the next page to make it your own.

MILLENNIUM

My marriage to Jerome Maugham admittedly was a failure. Never could I reach him. Perhaps he would say the same of me. I do not know. We never discussed it. There was nothing, in fact, we did discuss.

I did not love Jerome. I thought once I did, when we married and set up our home outside of London in the year of our Lord 994, but I was wrong. Under the same roof we went our separate ways. I looked after Stuart, our son, as Jerome became more and more wrapped up in his study of religion.

Sometimes, late at night, I looked in on him. He would be reading, shuffling through a pile of manuscripts, his thin shoulders hunched, his eyes intense with religious fervor. He looked for all the world like a miser hoarding money. More and more he lived in the past.

Maybe, had I tried harder, I could have made a success of my marriage to Jerome. In the first year I did try, before the birth of our son. A bride of fifteen, I set my ideals too high. I looked upon Jerome, at twenty-two, as a man of sophistication. But he was not. He cared about little but his studies, working the fields by day and burning the lamps by night. Often, days would pass with hardly a word between us.

Maybe, too, had Stuart not been so afflicted, requiring constant care, I could have devoted more attention to Jerome. But then, I suppose, it became too late. I was filled with good reasons, which by light of day became excuses.

Jerome decided that Stuart and I would accompany him on the end of the world pilgrimage to Jerusalem. Despite official denouncement by the church itself, there was a growing belief throughout England that the millennium mentioned in Revelation XX of the Holy Scriptures would occur on the New Year's Eve. There would be great happiness as the risen Christ took His rightful place and ruled the earth. Men, women and children clustered throughout England to join thousands of other pilgrims, including serfs and knights, bound for the long journey to Mount Zion.

Stuart's condition being as it was, I fought against going. Jerome insisted that there was a strong possibility of Stuart's being healed. No, not a possibility, a conviction.

Almost since infancy, Stuart had been afflicted. Despite many attempts to disguise the fact from Jerome, from Stuart, and most of all from myself, Stuart's condition seemed to worsen with each passing day.

"He'll outgrow it," I'd tell Jerome. "A great many children outgrow it." Jerome would look at me quizzically. He said nothing.

Stuart would suddenly lose consciousness. Then there would be a series of spasms throughout his body. Afterwards, he would fall into a heavy sleep that lasted for hours. It would be so deep he'd appear to be dead.

Were I finally able to rouse him, he would be extremely irritable, striking out blindly. Sometimes, too, were I not careful, Stuart would awaken from his sleep, or rather *seem* to do so, then wander off. Often he became lost. If anyone questioned him, he wouldn't or couldn't answer. If touched accidentally by others while in this state, Stuart sometimes flew into a rage, beating on them unmercifully.

Fortunately, at the age of five, he was not a large child. However, I could not see us going on such a trip as Jerome proposed. I knew it would be an almost impossible task to manage Stuart. Jerome attempted to reassure me.

"Suppose Stuart has a spell? How will we keep up with the group?" I asked.

"I'll carry him," Jerome responded. "You'll see."

"Why do you *want* to go?" I asked.

"I have to," Jerome answered.

"Sometimes when Stuart has a spell," I objected, "he soils himself."

"We'll carry extra clothing for him."

Seeing my look, he interpreted it correctly. "Oh, I'll carry those too."

Against my better judgment, hoping for a reprieve in some unknown fashion, I reluctantly prepared for the journey, perhaps as a recompense for not loving Jerome. We each took one change of clothing, and, of course, our capes. It would be too difficult to carry more.

Many not going on the pilgrimage reaped a plentiful harvest as they purchased bargains in furniture, clothing, livestock and homes. The pilgrims sold them cheaply or gave them away in order to guarantee themselves a place in paradise. They were aware of how a rich man is likened to a camel going through a needle's eye.

"'Behold the lilies of the field,'" said some of the holy men as they asked for the money the pilgrims had received. "'They toil not, neither do they spin.' You will need none of this. Trust in the Lord. He will take care of you."

Only much later did I discover that many such holy men were themselves remaining behind.

Some pilgrims decided to forgive debts. Merchants, confessing to having cheated customers, gave their money to the holy men as a form of bribery to secure forgiveness. Cautious pilgrims, thinking they could return to their homes if the last judgment did not occur, disposed of nothing. They were in the minority.

"Oh, ye of little faith," taunted the holy men.

Jerome insisted on selling or giving away everything. I, however, appealed to my mother to buy our little cottage for a pittance.

"I'll keep it for you, Vida," she said. "If you return, it will be waiting, just as you left it."

Mother refused to accompany us. She prepared a tasty meal of beef and kidney pie, vegetables and rich desserts, kissed us and gave us her blessing.

But the effects of the food did not last long, and soon our stomachs were empty. We learned that singing disguised the hunger and helped us cover ground quickly.

"There are angels in the sky. In the clouds—with shining trumps. See the angels?" my neighbor shouted.

I saw no angels. Only clouds.

"We shall march, even as the children of Israel marched," Jerome announced. "There shall be a pillar of fire before us by night, a pillar of smoke by day."

"You don't really believe that, do you?" I asked him. He did not reply.

"God summons us to His Day of Judgment," another pilgrim declared. "For is it not written that God shall reign for one thousand years over a new earth?"

"The Spirits of the Holy Apostles shall lead us through deep valleys and over high mountains," a third pilgrim said.

"Oh, yes," another joined in. "We shall live as they lived so long ago."

"Before we reach our goal," one of the holy men continued, "some of you may die. But have no fear. For those who die are blessed. Their souls shall prepare a place for those of us who follow."

The holy man was right. By the thousands the marchers died from starvation, exposure and illness. First were the elderly and those with afflictions.

The journey seemed endless. To pass the time, I taught psalms and canticles to Stuart. Jerome was true to his word. He carried our son, often lingering behind when Stuart had fits. At first the weather was balmy and warm. Quickly, autumn was upon us. At night we shivered, stretched out on the ground, huddled close for warmth.

Some superstitious folk looked upon Stuart as being possessed by Satan. Others disagreed; they claimed him blessed by God, seeing visions denied the rest of us.

Sometimes our band divided; one segment went one way, the rest another. Sometimes we met groups coming from other villages and towns. At times it was necessary for carts traveling to market to take to the fields as we straggled past. After a time, the villages all looked alike, and all we could contemplate was the next step we would take and the next.

Over rivers and through mountainous country we journeyed. A few were lost in the raging waters that nearly swept us off our feet. I grasped Jerome more tightly around the waist and followed his sure-footed progress. Malnourished and weak, we began to rest more often for longer and longer periods.

Across high ranges covered with forests and vineyards, their summits castle-crowned, we struggled. Under other circumstances I might have paused to view the colored leaves on the trees or the lightly falling snow. Instead, these hurried us on our way, foretelling of the hardships of approaching winter. In each meadow through which we passed the crows cawed noisily, their voices seeming to call, "Fool, fool, you. Fool."

Bit by bit, I became accustomed to what I saw. I stared at my surroundings less and less while those we passed stared at us. My once-lovely clothing was soiled and shoddy, as was that of all the pilgrims. I resented the shabbiness.

Sometimes farmers pressed upon us the produce from their fields, apologetic for not joining the pilgrimage. Others scoffed at us, calling us dreamers and fanatics.

I wished I could leave the pilgrimage and remain on some pleasant spot, but from childhood it had been impressed on me that a wife's place is beside her husband. In my bitterness, blaming Jerome, yet not saying a thing to him, I suspect I showed my frustrations in other ways. Poor man. He took all I did without complaint.

Every time there was a heavy storm, the sighting of a meteor, a minor trembling of the earth, or a high wind, there was panic among the pilgrims. Frightened, weeping, everywhere people asked one another: "Is it happening?"

"God is angry," said some, hearing thunder. Falling to their knees, rain pelting down upon them, they sought God's grace with outstretched arms.

"Our Father, Who art in heaven," they prayed, "forgive us if we have offended Thee."

Finally, Jerome told me we had arrived in Mount Zion. As we climbed to the top, I saw that many friends and neighbors who had started the journey were absent. Some, I know, had dropped out to return home. Most of the missing had died en route. My eyes filled with tears.

A hush descended on the throng as we knelt and prayed. It reminded me in an insane way of how an audience conducts itself while waiting for a group of strolling players to begin their performance after all have assembled.

But the show did not begin.

"They didn't figure time in Biblical days like they do today," said the holy men.

So we waited for days on end for Jesus to come. The old year ended; the new began.

Disheartened, disenchanted, many families began the long trip back. Some talked of settling in communities they had seen along the way, rather than facing the comments they expected at home. Others felt that since God had not judged them, they might as well have a good time until He did.

Jerome was depressed. He realized that he had insisted on bringing Stuart and me from the relative comforts of home through unspeakable hardship for no useful purpose whatever.

"Mother will let us have our cottage back," I finally told him, hoping to cheer him up a bit as we walked along. He refused to be cheered.

On our way home, Stuart had one spell after another. Jerome improvised a sling to carry him. Still we lagged behind. As we traveled through a mountainous region, Stuart had a violent seizure in Jerome's arms. He flailed about wildly, kicking and hitting at his father. I tried to calm him, and his violence only increased.

Jerome made a misstep on the narrow path. Stuart in his arms, he tumbled down the precipice. I saw them sprawled at the bottom, far below. Stuart had landed on the bundle of supplies and appeared unhurt. Jerome's body lay crumpled and still.

"Jerome," I called. "Jerome, answer me. Are you all right?"

I knew the words were inane. I could tell he was not all right. He responded with a groan that reached me at the top of the cliff.

"I'll get somebody," I called. Then I yelled wildly to the pilgrims in the distance. No one bothered to answer.

I slid and stumbled down the mountainside.

"I tried," Jerome gasped, unable to rise. "Oh, God, Vida, you'll never know how I tried."

I pillowed his head in my arms. He told me how his father, his grandfather, his uncle and his brother all had spells similar to Stuart's. He told me I shouldn't reproach myself. Instead, he was the one to blame in never having told me.

"There were many things I should have told you," he said. "Such as how much I love you. You never thought I did, I know, but I loved you more than anybody in the world."

"Shhh," I said. "I know now. Save your strength."

"How is Stuart? Is he hurt?"

"I'll see," I said and looked at my son. "He's sleeping peacefully. You cushioned his fall."

Jerome opened his eyes. A slight trickle of blood appeared on his lips. I wiped it away and kissed him.

"I see it now," he whispered.

"What is it you see?" I asked.

"The last judgment. The last judgment." He gasped, shuddered slightly and died in my arms.

As vultures circled, I gathered stones to cover his body. Perhaps I was too numb with fatigue to feel much of anything.

I bent down and picked up Stuart. "Sleep, baby, sleep," I whispered. He looked serene in my arms. I discarded some of our belongings and managed to carry Stuart to the path from which he and Jerome had tumbled.

The procession was nowhere to be seen. Perhaps when they rested, I'd be able to overtake them.

Hurrying to catch up, I was waylaid by a gang of ruffians. One of them took Stuart from my arms and laid him down. They said they were going to rob me. I told them I had nothing, but they refused to believe me. When they found it was true, they hit me, knocking me down.

I glanced at Stuart, who lay nearby, his face pressed into the ground. Crawling toward him, I tried to gather him up. One of the men laughed and told me Stuart was dead. I refused to believe him. Yet when I examined him more closely, I saw that it was true.

I tried to bury him as best I could, as I had Jerome. Then I made my way back to my native village. The little cottage where we had lived was in ruin. Mother was nowhere to be found. There were famine and plague. Thousands of people were dying throughout the land. I knew I would soon be one of them.

5. ANALYZING YOUR STORY

Along with adapting the story to fit your own particular needs, you'll want to be certain you have figured out everything necessary to presenting it well. This means analyzing it.

It's a good idea to write out the analysis so you can follow along with it when you're practicing the delivery. I think it helps to type out the story triple-spaced, so you have plenty of room to write on the copy and indicate important elements you've discovered. This same copy can also serve as your "plan of delivery," which you will want to refer to as you're learning the story. You can keep it handy, as a kind of security blanket, up till the first time you tell the story; though, of course, you should long be past needing to refer to it before you ever appear before an audience.

STEPS IN STORY ANALYSIS

Characterization

There are many different steps in the analysis. The first thing you may want to spend time with is your characterization. Much like writers or actors, you need to understand the characters. In a large number of told stories, such as fables, characters are simple and there's little to do in understanding them. But this isn't always the case.

Important Traits and Background

The more complicated the characters, the more time you need to spend with them. This is so you can convey their essence to your listeners. First, you need to figure out their important traits in order to be true to them in your presentation. Later, you'll want to figure out how to use your body and voice to convey the character traits to an audience.

Unless the story is an extremely simple fable, such as "The Guilty Woman" or "Repaying Good with Evil," you may want to spend some time figuring out what in the character's background has made the person as he or she is. Certainly, most stories don't express this sort of thing explicitly; rather, it's through inference. But when you discover important sections that either explain character or any other facets of the story, you'll want to be sure to emphasize them for an audience. You can't, of course, if you haven't done your homework.

The more you know about the characters and the story as a whole, the more chance you have of presenting the story convincingly and truthfully.

Emotions

In addition to personality traits, you need to determine the emotions of your characters. What are they feeling during each part of the story? And, it helps, of course to understand why they are experiencing these feelings. You may need to go back to the background analysis you just did to determine the answer. Or it may be apparent, particularly with simple characterizations, from the context. The hunter in "The Guilty Woman" is angry because someone has taken his dinner. In our culture, his actions in finding out who the thief is seem extreme. But when we take into consideration the entire framework of the story, the **general background**, if you will, then it is easy to accept. It has to do with the story's **framework**. Once a certain frame of reference is established, you, as the teller, and your listener should be willing to accept it. In "Zepheriah and the Mighty Mini," which comes later in this chapter, there's a facetious reference made to framework. The point is, however, that anything is OK if its possibility is set up ahead of time.

Motives

Another part of character analysis is figuring out motives. All characters in the story are there for a reason; they have a particular goal they want to reach, either overall in their lives or only in the context of the story. You need to figure out what these motives are. Much of the motivation, like the emotion, comes from something in the characters' backgrounds.

The Wise Man in "Repaying Good with Evil" comes across as a decent sort of person, so his motivation at first is to do good. This story is different from many in that the entire tale centers around this motive, which is tested repeatedly until the man is forced to change his beliefs. In most stories, you don't have a change of personality as you do here. Rather, you learn more about the character as the story progresses. What the person does may come as a surprise, but it is also consistent with what has gone before.

Characters' motives are directly related to their relationships with each other. And the kinds of relationships they have are important to the plot or to the unfolding of the story. A story with a plot, in effect, portrays motives coming into conflict. The two major characters, the hero or protagonist and the anti-hero or antagonist, each want something, and their desires cause a clash. This in turn is related to the story's purpose, what it is saying.

The following is a nostalgia piece centering around the old woman. Mrs. Bigelow not only is important to the story, she *is* the story, which, of course, is a character study.

What can you figure out about her? What are her traits? Which of them are most important to the story? Why? What are her motives? Does she, in fact, have any real motive here? Why or why not? What does she want? Where is the conflict?

Until the end, the only characters besides Mrs. Bigelow are her husband and daughter, who actually appear only in her mind. So they aren't real; they're only as she perceives them. It's an idealized view. Yet you need to figure out what she thinks they are like so you can try to present them this way. Obviously, she had, or thought she had, a good relationship with them. How would you describe it?

Often, much of a story's interpretation is up to you, the teller. And what you determine may be vastly different from what someone else sees. But that's OK, as long as you can justify your choice.

What can you tell about the two other characters, Beth and Jim Ames? Even though they are simply devices to explain what happened, you still have to analyze them to a degree to make them believable. Maybe you can figure out why Jim was against inviting Mrs. Bigelow, so it's clear in your mind. In that way you can better make the story believable. Remember that the audience doesn't have to see the same motives as you do, but they have to be convinced you are presenting the story truthfully.

A REMEMBRANCE OF CHRISTMAS PAST

Old Mrs. Bigelow opened her purse and counted out $1.19. Picking up the pound of hamburger, she turned and shuffled from the store. She'd go home, maybe listen to the radio and then go to bed. She'd get up about six-thirty, eat half a piece of toasted bread and drink a cup of very sweet tea. Then she'd putter around until it was time for lunch. She'd fix a meatloaf. Use the whole pound of meat. She usually managed to stretch that much hamburger over three or four meals. But tomorrow, after all, was Christmas, a special day. She had a right to be extravagant.

Special day indeed! But it used to be—when Mary was little; when Tom was alive.

The old woman opened the door to the small, frame house and switched on the light in the kitchen. She put the meat in the refrigerator and took off her hat and coat. Pulling a chair out from the table, she sat down and switched on the radio. At first all she got was static. She quit fiddling with the dial when she heard the soft strains of "Silent night, holy night."

Christmas Eve! It used to be the best time of all. There was such excitement. She always baked cookies then. She knew it was silly, but she never seemed to get to it before that. Mary would watch in wide-eyed wonder as the soft dough was changed into beautiful shapes of stars and angels and put into the oven where it would become sweet, crunchy cookies.

Soon she'd hear Tom stomp up the steps, pausing to kick off his boots. He'd burst through the door, carrying a scraggly pine tree he'd tramped miles through the woods to cut.

"Emma, it really isn't much, but it's the best I could do," he'd say.

"Oh, Tom, it's beautiful! The nicest tree we've ever had."

"Do you think so?"

"It's perfect. Just the right size."

Mary would dance in circles, shouting, "Daddy, daddy, daddy."

The old woman sighed. It still didn't seem real—Tom being dead, and Mary out in California, the other side of the country.

She angrily brushed a tear from her eye. "My goodness," she chided herself, "self-pity at your age?" Then she smiled as she tried to force her thoughts back to those Christmas Eves long ago.

Yes, now she remembered. After they'd admired the tree, they'd sit down to supper. Mary would be all excited, and it would be nearly impossible to get her to sleep. After she was settled, the real fun began.

Talking in whispers, she and Tom would dig the ornaments out of the attic and trim the tree. Or did they fill the stocking first? Oh, Lord, she couldn't remember.

She shivered, got up and limped to the closet. She pulled out a tattered sweater, put it across her shoulders and sat down again. She glanced at the cuckoo clock above the sink. Nearly ten. She supposed she'd have to go to bed soon. But she didn't want to sleep. It was much more pleasant to sit and think.

She sighed and closed her eyes. She became aware of a voice singing "Little Town of Bethlehem." That was Tom's favorite.

Suddenly, she remembered. They always filled the stocking first.

She stood up painfully. She had to be sure there was an orange in the toe. And Tom might forget. She went to the pantry. Only she felt different now, not stiff and old. She glanced at her hands. They were young, strong.

"Don't forget the orange, honey."

She turned, startled. Tom stood by the door, smiling at her. Not the emaciated Tom of a few years ago, but the laughing, bright-eyed Tom.

She ran toward him and threw her arms around his neck.

"Hey, what is this? All I did was remind you about the oranges."

"My dearest." She kissed his forehead, his mouth, his cheeks. "How I've missed you."

"Missed me? Why I haven't been anywhere, Emma. Just out getting my boots. Don't want some dog carrying them off."

Emma shook her head. She couldn't understand. But why should she try? It was wonderful to have Tom back. And Mary?

She ran to the bedroom. Yes, there she was, sound asleep, her Teddy bear clutched to her chest. My goodness, that old teddy bear! Emma hadn't seen it in years.

She tiptoed back to the kitchen. Tom was already filling the stocking. She laughed and ran a hand through his thick, black hair.

They quickly finished. Emma got two cups and filled them with eggnog. She carried them to the living room and handed one to Tom. They sat on the couch, their bodies touching, the warmth spreading from one to the other. Emma raised the cup to her lips. There was a crash.

The next day Beth and Jim Ames came by to ask old Mrs. Bigelow next door for dinner, a spur of the moment invitation.

They knocked, but there was no answer.

"Maybe she's ill," Jim said.

"Do you suppose we should see?"

Jim tried the door. It swung open, and they entered the kitchen. The only sounds were the ticking of a cuckoo clock above the sink and an occasional spitting noise from an ancient radio on the table.

Jim walked into the living room. Old Mrs. Bigelow lay back on the couch, her eyes closed and a smile on her face. The rug nearby was stained with water. A broken glass lay near the old woman's feet.

Theme

For an overall understanding of the story, you need to figure out what you think is the theme. Theme is what the story means overall, what it's saying to the audience. You should be able to state this in simple terms such as: Crime doesn't pay ("The Guilty Woman") or, Even a good man's patience reaches a breaking point ("Repaying Good with Evil").

Conceivably, you could come up with different interpretations of the theme than others would. In some stories the theme is apparent. But often you have to examine a story quite closely to determine what it is.

There's no sure way to know what's "correct," but if you can support your idea through material in the story, then you've done your job.

The following story exists just for fun, for entertainment. Yet, even the "fluffiest" of tales has some sort of central idea. Otherwise, there would be no coherence to it. (The only exception is total nonsense material that uses made-up words.) What do you think is the theme of this story?

ZEPHERIAH AND THE MIGHTY MINI

Zepheriah Thompson was frustrated and so bit down hard on the tip of his finger. Especially fitted for work with the Mighty Mini-XPMP33910 Computer, his finger, therefore, was encased in hard but flexible cryptonic lead, the best conductor to date for the tensile tales that poured forth from Zephie's brain and into his finger and hence into the Mighty Mini-X.

It was a dumb thing to do. Cryptonic lead was the strongest substance known to woman (man, too, as a matter of fact) and couldn't be dented or marred. Cracked and crumbling enamel rained down on the legs and knees of Zephie's gold metallic jumpsuit and fluttered down to the living room rug, which opened its tiny piles and gobbled up the unexpected treat.

"Oh, wow," Zephie said to himself. "Gee willikers, darn." He was upset, you see, because reconstructive oral surgery would now be necessary. And that would delay him even more. "It's a real bummer," he said to no one in particular because no one in particular was there. No one in general, either, for Zephie was very much alone, isolated to complete his work. "I mean it's like poopies, man, that I can't get myself moving," he articulated. "I, the greatest writer of twenty-cent thrillers in the business. I, whom the Emperor of North Eurasica called his favorite talesman."

Zephie pushed the "E" for experience button on the Mighty-Mini and was surrounded and filled with his creation. Only a little of his former consciousness, his link to the present, remained. He had otherwise transported himself to the world of his own creation. Well, not wholly his, he thought. There were those faceless figures from afar, those featureless phantoms from the past. Those twenty-cent men and women about whom Zephie was the world's foremost authority. "Twenty-seven skidoo," he told himself, "and Solid Johnson, I know more about them than any other living person. It was I, Zepheriah, who pored through old books. It was my nose-cone that was exposed to mildew and crumbling paper. It was my breathing apparatus that failed to filter and gave me a stopped-up nose."

Now his present predicament had caused him to have another stopped-up nose. (Actually, not another. It was the same nose but stopped up once more.) He covered his face-plate with his hands, scraping it with the cryptonite alloy on his finger, as tears ran down his cheeks and were gently sucked away by his self-contained waste-disposal and purifying system. "Beastly," he wailed. "Just beastly. What am I to do?" He snuffed a big snuff of very pure air. "I can't afford to equus around like this. I've got to get the zinc out."

The world he'd created was fast evaporating, as were the tears on his cheeks, the drippings from his runny nose. "I'll bet I look like... What is it? What is it I look like?" He shook his head in frustration. "Unmannerly-dolf, the red-nosed precipitation-elk." He paused and then sobbed. "No, no, no! That's not it. I can't think. I just can't think." He sobbed once more.

Well, gentle listener, what do you suppose is causing Zephie's problems? The clues are there. Can you solve the mystery?

Yes, just as you suspected, he has...no, not exactly "writer's block." For you see, dear listener, in Zephie's time there are no writers. There are tale creators. Technology has progressed to the point where emotions and worlds and physical sensations and perceptions can be imposed directly on the...no, not "reader." "Receiver," perhaps. "Groker," maybe.

You, tender listener, being attuned to the cosmic consciousness, grasp the idea. Zephie's stuck. Despite all the resources at his command, he can't finish his tale. And so he'll be exiled by the emperor. To frozen wastelands or burning planets. Perhaps he'll go where no man has dared been sent before. The last frontier. You guessed it. Jersey City. Ah, cruel fate.

Should we go back to Zephie's childhood to see what has caused him to become thus blocked?

Zephie was the elder of two children, the first born in his city in 474 years. People had longer lifespans then, you see, and overpopulation was a problem.

He weighed in at 8 pounds, 7 ounces. A chubby little guy with dimples, one on each of his four cheeks. His was an ordinary infancy. Two o'clock feedings. The usual robo-nanny. By the time he was ten months old, he'd said his first word. "Antidisestablishmentarianism." By twelve months he was speaking in phrases. At eighteen months he'd written his first story. It was about a spider who was deathly afraid of flies. This was somewhat astounding in that flies and spiders had long since been eliminated from the earth.

The answer, of course, was that Zepheriah, already at this tender age, had launched himself on the path toward scholarly investigation into the twentieth century. He had an inquiring mind, an honest-to-goodness twenty-cent mentality.

Since he was such a cute little mite, a precocious child, in a world where children were rare, he was doted upon and pampered. Thus he found it easy to talk his robo-nanny into getting more and more environment-creation tapes for him to experience, those both factual and fictional in nature. But when he ran out—he was a fast assimilator—he searched the furthest archives and dusty shelves of the environment-brary. There he found and examined environment-simulator tapes, feelies, smellies, and videos.

At two he entered first form and progressed through eighteenth, graduating when he was ten. Along the way his robo-nanny, no longer really essential, began to spend more and more time with her ro-boyfriend. Inevitably, he and Zephie met. Now it so happened that this self-same ro-boyfriend was valet and shoeshine expert for a highly respected thriller talesman. Zephie showed the taler some of the things he'd written, and the man told him to "bug off, creep." Not one to be discouraged, however, he kept at it. Experiencing and creating. Soon he was flooding the market, and his tales had a twist. They were twenty-cent and the world was hungry to learn of earlier days.

Immensely successful, Zephie still wasn't happy, however. He had an unfulfilled ambition. It was to be greater even than the most respected and popular tellers of tales, Brad Brinbury and H. Hider Ragged.

Zephie had set his goal and so proceeded. But then he became blocked.

Are you curious to see how Zephie solves his problem? Well, Brad and H. Hider sneak into his environment one night and tie him to a newly-created railroad track. Laughing hysterically, they run off in seventeen directions. (Anything's possible if the format is established!) Five freight trains, a hand-pushed fruit cart and three elephants with earmuffs race toward him with or without the thought of bodily harm. Suddenly, out of nowhere, a masked man appears. He's wearing a trench coat, dangly, gold earrings, and a polka dot hanky over his mouth and nose. On his head is a red cap with a brown plume. Yes, he's the famous humanitarian criminal, THE MAN WHO CLIMBS THROUGH UPSTAIRS BEDROOM WINDOWS and steals wooden nickels to give to the poor. It's... Actually, up to this point, Zephie's problem has been how to become unblocked, not untied. This new man doesn't fit this tale at all. And if I told you about him, it would be...(Ready?)...just a *second story*, man!

A good test of whether or not you understand the theme of the story is to try to state it in a short paragraph of no more than three simple sentences. If you can do that, you can be sure you have it pretty well in mind.

In a well-constructed story, everything that is included should relate to the central idea or theme. If you're preparing to tell a story and find some elements that don't fit, you'd better either examine the work more carefully to see where you've gone wrong, or, if you're sure that the parts don't fit, then cut them out.

Mood

There are a number of other things you should determine. Earlier, I talked about figuring out how the characters feel. Their emotions may be and usually are different from the overall feeling or mood of the story.

Usually, a story has one predominant mood that is important to convey to your listeners. Just as with theme, another teller could come up with a predominant mood that is different from the one you chose. Again, it depends on your interpretation. For "A Remembrance of Christmas Past," the predominant mood might be one of longing because throughout Mrs. Bigelow wants to recapture earlier Christmas celebrations, going so far as to make herself believe she has gone back in time. Or it could be one of sorrow or even pity in the listeners' reactions to the events.

Go back to the earlier stories in this book and try to figure out what you think is the predominant mood, the feeling you want to leave with your listeners when you've finished. Justify your choices.

Organization of Plot

A very important aspect of your analysis is figuring out how the story is organized. In any tale that has a plot, there is an inciting incident, rising action, and a climax.

Plotted stories are the most common, the most traditional. This is so because our interest is maintained through the anticipation of the outcome and how it will be accomplished. A story holds

95

our attention because of its unfolding and its revelations. In other words, it keeps us in suspense.

Protagonist and Antagonist

A plot revolves around the meeting of two opposing forces, the protagonist and the antagonist. Both want something, and in trying to reach their goals they come up against each other. Their struggle continues until one of them is overcome.

The protagonist is almost always a human being (or in fables and myths, an animal or god with human characteristics) and so is the antagonist. Sometimes, however, the antagonist can be a force of nature, such as a bad storm, or else the forces of society. It can also be the protagonist struggling against self.

During your analysis, you need to figure out who is your protagonist and who or what is the antagonist. Is it society, as in "Zepheriah and the Mighty Mini X," where a man is pitted against conditions he has trouble accepting? Is it another person (or animal), as in "Repaying Good with Evil"? Here, at first, the conflict seems to be between the man and the serpent but quickly changes so that the real antagonist is the coyote. Is it a person against self, as in the excerpt about the strangling? At first, similar to "Repaying Good with Evil," the conflict seems to be between Martin and his father. But it quickly changes in that, because of the conditions of his life, Martin is unhappy. Then the conditions of having to live at home appear to be the antagonist. But they're not. His real struggle is whether or not he can go on. Part of him wants to live; part of him wants to die. He is struggling with himself.

Inciting Incident

At any rate, a story begins with a particular balance, or the balance has been upset shortly before the story begins. In "The Rescue," the upset occurs when the little girl discovers that the cat has captured the chipmunk. Yet the chipmunk's story is subordinate to that of the girl's. The conflict is whether or not she can keep the chipmunk.

The upset is the **inciting incident,** that which is responsible for the opposition beginning. A problem now has to be solved before life can return to normal for the protagonist.

In any story with a plot, you need to figure out the inciting incident so you can make sure it isn't lost to your listeners. If it is, they may as well not hear the rest of the story.

Rising Action, Turning Point, and Climax

Once the inciting incident occurs, there is rising action. In many a story from the oral tradition, the solving of one problem leads directly to another. The big, bad wolf first destroys the house of straw, then the house of wood, and then tries to destroy the house of brick. Each of these episodes includes a high point for the action. In any story, you need to figure out where these high points occur so you can emphasize them for an audience, so you can, through body and voice, create more tension and suspense, until you reach a high point in your delivery. This is the turning point and climax, the place where the protagonist either wins or loses.

Along the sides of your copy of the story you can indicate where these changes occur, so you can learn them along with learning the progression of the story. Then you can determine how to convey them to an audience.

Stories That Have No Plot

Maybe a story you tell has no plot. Still you have to figure out the high points, the punch lines, if you will. Just as in a joke, these are the lines that actually do need punching or pointing up. In "Threshing Day," the high points are:

1) when the threshing machine arrives;

2) the narrator's "wanting to get into the act" and then helping;

3) the narrator's being called to help prepare the table for lunch;

4) the day's ending with the sound of the wheels mingled with that of the dishes.

These are the most important parts—in other words, a kind of outline or skeleton, the bones being the main supporting points.

In "The Creation" the important points would correspond with what the Bible tells us God did in creating the world. Some of the high points would be God's throwing the ball of dirt to create the earth, using the squirt gun to give the earth water, using a cat-o'-

nine-tail to create the sun and stars, and so on. You need to figure out these parts of a story so that they are not lost to the listener.

Universality

One of the major steps in analyzing your story is figuring out if it has universality. Most likely, if it's a story that's been handed done from one generation to another, it does, or it wouldn't continue to survive. Universality means that the story has meaning for everyone; that is, it relates in some way to the human condition and to our wants and needs.

We need to be able to take the characters and their problems and relate them to something in our own lives. Universality is tied in with theme, what the story means. Part of its success depends not on what it says but on what it doesn't say—what it makes you think or feel. It should make you go beyond the actual words in its relevance to your life.

Symbolism

Part of this going beyond actual words is included in the symbolism the stories use. Fables and myths in particular contain situations and characters who are symbols for everyone. In many cases, they are not very individualized. They have few, if any, distinguishing traits. This makes them more universal, more symbolic of everyone who comes in contact with them.

Imagery

Even though a told story usually doesn't have long passages of description, what it does have should be important. These passages should go much beyond the words themselves in making you visualize or taste or smell. Because of this you need to point them out. Let the audience hear the leaves crinkling on the path Hansel and Gretel take; let them smell the gingerbread. Part of your analysis should be making the imagery clear.

Voice

On the paper where you've copied your story, you may want to indicate how a particular passage should be spoken, using such devices as voice quality, rate, and vocal variety. These things will be discussed in detail in a later chapter. You may want to indicate pauses by using / for short pauses and // for longer ones.

In the beginnin' of time, /
Not your time,/ nor my time, //
but clear at first/ when things started happenin', //
God said to himself, //
"I'm gonna have a little fun, /
I'm gonna create Me a world."

You may want to pick out and underline key words and phrases, to make sure the audience hears them.

One day the chipmunk was running along the wall when plop, a soft paw came down on him and held him fast. A large, yellow cat had caught him. He wiggled and wiggled, but could not get free.

Use of Words

Of course, you also should be familiar with all the words in the story. If there are any important ones that you don't know, look up their meaning and their pronunciation, even if you are going to change them. Because in order to choose synonyms, you have to know what the original words mean.

The more you understand your story, the more chance you have of making it meaningful for an audience. So it's a good idea to go through the steps discussed in addition to considering anything else you think is important.

Exercises

1. Take one of the stories from this book and analyze the characters in detail. Figure out their motives, their relationships to the other characters, and their purpose for being included.

2. Choose a story you think you'd like to tell and figure out its theme, its organization, and what makes it universal.

3. Copy a story you'd like to tell, and then go through it, picking out the important words and phrases, underlining them, and determining the use of pausing.

4. Find a story you do not especially like and try to determine why you don't like it. How could it be changed so you would like it?

6. LEARNING YOUR STORY

Learning a story to tell is not like memorizing a poem or lines in a play. Rather, you adapt the story to make it yours. Then you allow for changes that may be necessary because of the telling situation (such as interruptions or poor acoustics) and the audience's response.

Particularly if you are telling stories to children, you may have unexpected interruptions when they ask a question, want something clarified, disagree with you, or even argue about something you've said.

What you do is learn the **essence** of the story, the broad outline. If certain lines are important (as are the punchlines in the three shaggy dog stories I used), then memorize those lines where you need to know exact wording. If you have a repeated phrase or magic words that must be said the same each time, you also need to memorize those. But if you attempt to memorize the whole story word for word, you may be asking for trouble.

THREE STEPS TO LEARNING YOUR STORY

1. Choose a Story You Like

The first thing you want to do is choose a story that you like. This may require a lot of thinking and consideration. Don't rush into it. I once rejected a story on first reading, then found it kept haunting me. But it was too late. I no longer had it and couldn't get it back.

When you read stories with the idea of learning them, don't be too quick to reject them. Although your first impression isn't good, the story may nag at you like the one I rejected. It was about killing a deer, which bothered me. That's why I returned it. Later, as I kept thinking about it, I realized that it had had a great impact on me, even though I was supposed to dislike the particular incident of the killing. On first reading, it had come across too powerfully for me to consider.

2. Determine the Sequence of Events

Suppose you've gone over several stories and finally settle on one. Then what? Well, the next step is pretty painless. Read it through a few times to be certain you've grasped everything important about it. Then put the story away for a day or two. During that time try to recall the sequence of events and the most important points.

Next, pick it up again, go through it, and consciously try once more to learn the sequence. Here it may help to make a list of these points, as you learned to do in the story analysis chapter. Let's take the following story for example.

THE ROOSTER WHO WOULD BE KING
told by Peninnah Schram

A long time ago, there lived a King and Queen and their son the Prince. They considered this prince to be their jewel, their greatest treasure—the apple of their eye. The King made certain that the Prince had the most learned teachers and the wisest soothsayers to instruct him in all that a prince would need to know in order to be a great king, when the time came for him to rule the kingdom.

One day, a strange illness overcame the Prince, and he began to act like a rooster. He took off his clothes and roamed all around the palace, flapping his arms like a rooster and crowing loud and long. He also stopped speaking the language of the King and Queen. He ate only corn from the floor, like a rooster, and refused to sit at the table with others, eating only *under* the table *alone*.

The King and Queen became very upset and called for the best doctors in the kingdom to treat the Prince, in hopes of curing him of his illness. But nothing that the doctors and the soothsayers and the other healers tried seemed to make any difference, and the Rooster Prince continued happily crowing and flapping his arms and hopping around in the palace, wherever he wanted to go.

One day, a wise old man came to the palace. "Your Majesty, I would like to try to cure the Prince," he said to the King.

"Where are your medicines?" asked the surprised King because all the doctors carried at least one bag filled with bottles of potions and pills.

"I have my own ways, Your Majesty," answered the wise man. "Allow me seven days *alone* with the Prince."

The King reluctantly agreed, since there was no other hope.

The wise man was brought to the Prince. The first thing he did was to take off all *his* clothing, jump under the table, and sit opposite the Rooster Prince. The Prince stared at the stranger for a very long time.

"Who are you, and what are you doing here?" crowed the Rooster Prince curiously.

"I am a rooster. Can't you see that?" answered the wise man matter-of-factly but patiently.

"Oh, I am a rooster, too. Welcome!" replied the Prince, happy to have found a friend.

Time passed with the two companions crowing and flapping their arms.

One day, the stranger got out from under the table and began to walk around—a little straighter each day. The Rooster Prince had grown so fond of his friend that he began to follow him wherever he went. And the two roosters hopped around the palace together.

On another day, the wise man put on a shirt and a pair of trousers. "What are you wearing, my friend?" asked the Rooster Prince. "Roosters don't wear clothes."

"You're right, dear Prince, but I was a bit chilled. However, I assure you, you can still be a good rooster even with clothes on. Try it!" challenged the wise man.

The Rooster Prince put some clothes on, too—and continued crowing and flapping his arms.

The next day, the wise man sat at the table and ate some corn from a golden platter. The Rooster Prince sat next to his friend. The wise man signaled to the servants, and soon the table was set with silverware, goblets, and golden plates. Slowly, the wise man began to eat all the delicious foods—in a proper manner—and the Prince began to imitate him. Soon a whole meal was eaten, and the Rooster Prince crowed most happily.

The following night, the wise man began to sleep on a bed. He again assured the Prince. "Don't worry, my Prince, you can be a good rooster just the same, even sleeping on a bed." And so the Rooster Prince resumed sleeping on his royal bed and no longer slept under the table.

Soon after, the wise man began to discuss the philosophy of life with the Prince. "Wait a minute, roosters don't have to think, and they certainly don't debate the merits of a way of life," declared the Prince. "Roosters just exist, being fed and cared for without any worries."

"You may be right," answered his wise old friend, "but on the other hand, it doesn't mean you can't be a good rooster if you do engage in discussion. After all, *you* will know that you are a rooster, just the same."

The Prince thought this over and began to discuss philosophical ideas with the wise man.

On the seventh day, the wise man bid farewell to the Prince. As he was about to leave, he said, "My friend, remember— roosters are fair game for the hunter. So always try to pretend you are a human prince. Act wisely and help others. Farewell!"

From that day on, the Prince walked, ate, and talked like the prince he was.

And when, in time, he became a great King ruling over that entire kingdom, no one besides himself knew that he was still a rooster.

You might write out the sequence of events, the high points, in the following way:

1. One day a prince began to act like a rooster.

2. His parents became very much concerned and called on the best doctors to treat him, but they failed.

3. A wise man came to the palace and said he'd like to have seven days in which to try to cure the prince.

4. When the king agreed to let the wise man try to cure his son, the wise man went to the prince and himself began acting like a rooster.

5. The prince was happy to have another rooster as a friend.

6. One day the wise man began to stand straight. The prince, who liked him, followed suit.

7. The wise man put on his clothing, telling the prince that even though roosters didn't wear clothes, he was chilly. The prince put on clothing.

8. The wise man sat at a table to eat, and the prince began to imitate him.

9. Next the wise man slept on a bed, and so did the prince.

10. The wise man began to discuss philosophy. When the prince objected that roosters didn't do that, the wise man said that he would still know he was a rooster if he did. The prince joined the discussion.

11. The next day the wise man prepared to leave, telling the prince that roosters are fair game for hunters, and he should pretend he's a prince.

12. The prince followed the wise man's advice and eventually became a great king. No one knew except the prince himself that he was still a rooster.

Of course, you will write this out in your own words, and you may add some things and omit others that I've included. It doesn't matter as long as it helps you remember the story. Now simply read over your list and try to get it firmly in mind. During the next day or so, keep going over it, even at odd moments: when you're brushing your teeth, when you're preparing for bed, when you driving by yourself.

3. Reread and Tell the Story to Yourself

Next reread the story. Then tell it to yourself, expanding on your written outline. Don't worry if you can't remember everything; you are learning.

Read it through and tell it to yourself as many times as is necessary. Each time you read it now, pay attention to colorful words and key phrases. Be sure you've done the analysis and know the characters as you know old friends. If you don't, go back over the story and try to figure out what they're like.

In some stories, such as the one about the rooster prince, there is little character description and little in the way of background. Still, you add your experiences to what you read and thus can make the characters real to yourself.

Generally, unless you're trying to tell a funny story, it's best to keep the plot and the characters simple. Lots of elaboration or ornamentation risks ruining the story.

Of course, in tall tales you may want a lot of detail. But this is the sort of thing that lends itself to improvisation. If you were telling about "Willie the Moth," much of the fun is relying on spur of the moment inspirations, maybe even suggested by audience members. So all you would learn is the bare outline. To tell this kind of story, of course, you have to be pretty comfortable in front of a group.

Keep in mind that you "learn" the story more completely each time you tell it, whether to yourself or to another person. So keep on telling it until you're confident you know it. Don't be surprised if, the first time you tell it to a friend or relative, you leave part of it out. This is only natural. Everyone does it.

If you're just beginning as a storyteller, it can help to tell the story several times on a one-to-one basis to gain confidence.

There is no right or wrong way either of learning a story or presenting it. If you want to write it out and memorize it, that's OK too, except it won't be quite as adaptable to different audiences and situations. It often helps to go over the story in your mind just before drifting off to sleep. That way, you'll tend to remember it better.

Take time to live with the story, and give yourself plenty of time to learn it. Then make it your own. Build the setting in your imagination. Know the characters as well as you can. Imagine the sensory stuff. Actually transport yourself into the story's imaginary realm. There are other tricks to learning the story, as well. You can tell it to your mirror image; you can record it, either on audio or video tape and then listen to it over and over.

TIPS AND TECHNIQUES

Vocal Inflection

As you become more certain with each story, you can begin to pay more attention to how you say it, rather than just saying it. Some people will tell you it's best to learn vocal inflection and so on right from the beginning. Others say it's best to get the ideas firmly in mind before you try anything fancy. As always, it depends on what works for you. At any rate, somewhere along the line you need to consider pauses, changes in vocal quality to indicate mood or character changes, and so on.

Movement

If you're a dancer or a mime to begin with, you may rely quite heavily on movement and so want to learn it right along with the oral part of the story. You can start to add gestures and movement, and experiment with different ways of standing and holding your body to indicate character and mood changes.

An important reminder as you're preparing your story: You don't have to act it out. You can simply let the language tell the story, unless, of course, you have a background in theatre or are confident you can pull it off. Then do whatever you like. The important thing is that your presentation should be effective. It doesn't matter whether you do more telling or acting if you accomplish your goal.

Cue Cards

If there are rhymes or chants or other exact words that need to be repeated, you can write these on cards, which you can use as a crutch in case you get lost.

I don't do this anymore, but for years when I appeared before an audience, either as a storyteller or actor, I hid my script somewhere on my person, either in a pocket or buttoned up inside my shirt. I knew that logically I couldn't take it out and refer to it if I blocked, but just having it next to me was enough.

If there are songs or poems you have to learn as part of the story, you might save them for later. It can give you a big boost to know that all you have yet to learn are ten or twelve lines of poetry, for instance.

Props

With many stories you can use properties, which can also serve as reminders of the events and what comes next. For example, in telling the story of the rooster prince, you may have drawings or cutouts. You can use all sorts of other props, from articles of clothing suggestive of the different characters to objects they each might possess. You don the clothing or pick up the object when you move from one section or one character to another.

The ideas for using props are only as limited as your imagination. For instance, professional storyteller Harlynne Geisler tells a story called "The Witch's House," intended for young kids. In *The Best of the Story Bag,* a booklet containing articles and short pieces from a monthly newsletter she writes and publishes, she outlines the story with the accompanying diagram.

THE WITCH'S HOUSE
told by Harlynne Geisler

O nce upon a time there was a tiny witch only three inches high who had a teeny cat only one inch high. The witch was very sad because it was Halloween, and she had no home to weave her spells in. As she walked down the street, she was hit in the face by a piece of paper. "Paper!" she exclaimed. "I can make a paper house." She took out her scissors and began to cut. She cut out an igloo shape and then a door for herself. Her cat mewed plaintively. "Oh, of course. You need a door too." So the witch cut out a little cat door and then a window to look out of. And it was the perfect house for a witch on Halloween: a jack-o'-lantern.

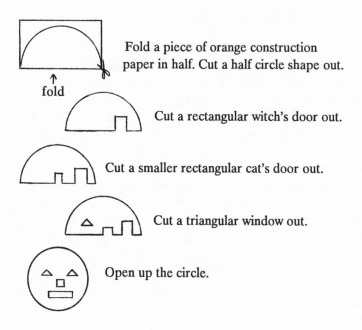

fold

Fold a piece of orange construction paper in half. Cut a half circle shape out.

Cut a rectangular witch's door out.

Cut a smaller rectangular cat's door out.

Cut a triangular window out.

Open up the circle.

FIGURE 6-1: A Halloween story / paper cutting

111

Geisler notes: "The story can be expanded to include the witch's search for a home—owl's nest, rabbit's hole, etc.—with her ejected from each one by the rightful owner who tells her that witches don't live in nests, etc. Both witch and cat can be given names too."

OTHER TELLERS' STORIES

If you are going to tell an authored story, you can either read or memorize it because you shouldn't deviate from the author's words, unless you're given permission. (Incidentally, I give you permission to do so with stories of mine that are printed in this book).

To Read Or To Memorize?

There are both advantages and disadvantages to either method. There are some who feel that you should read the story, since having the manuscript in front of you constantly reminds the listener that the words you are using aren't your own.

The disadvantages of reading are that you have to look down so much that you lose eye contact with the listener. Also, the book you use can set up a physical barrier between you and the audience.

An advantage of reading is that although you take as much time to analyze the story and spend a great deal of time practicing it, you don't have to go to the trouble of actually learning it. You also don't run as much risk of getting lost as you do when you forget the story you are telling. Of course, if you do get lost, it will interrupt the reading while you try to find your place, but you have the security of knowing that sooner or later you'll find where you left off.

There are advantages to memorizing an authored story: you don't need to lose eye contact with the audience, and there is no physical barrier.

But there are disadvantages to memorization, too. Everyone has had the experience of forgetting what comes next, no matter how well they think they know something. And if you've memorized rather than simply learned a story, it's much more difficult to get going again once you've stopped. If, when telling a story you've memorized, you suffer a momentary block, you may be able to think through your outlined sequence and get back on track. But if you can't recall the specific words, it may be disastrous.

The best storytelling situation exists when the listener cannot separate the teller from the story. You can create the illusion of this with memorized words, but you can't actually achieve it.

Whether memorizing or reading, you are doing what is known as *oral interpretation.* You are taking something that already exists in final form and interpreting it the way you see it for an audience. No matter how well the work is presented, it really can't be as intimate an experience as simply telling a story. The reason is that you need to adhere strictly to the author's words, instead of your own, and your words are bound to be at least somewhat different from the author's.

Tips for Memorization

The steps to learning a story and actually memorizing it are similar, except that you'll likely spend much more time in the learning stage. There is no method of memorization that works best for everyone.

Some people go over the story first to learn the sequence of events and the main points, just as they would in learning a story to tell. Then they concentrate on actual words and phrases. Others simply read the story a few times to gain a sense of what it says, without actually bothering to memorize the sequence first.

No matter how you try to memorize the story, the process will be a tedious one. A method that seems to work for some people is to keep going over and over the entire story, saying as much of it aloud each time as can be remembered, then reading it some more and trying to fill in previous gaps.

Here's the way I do it. I memorize the first sentence (or part of a sentence), say it either to myself or aloud a few times, memorize the second sentence, say the first and second together, add the third, and so on, always going over the story from the beginning to as far as I've memorized.

Certainly, you can memorize and present your own written stories. But here again you run into problems in that you cannot adapt the story for different audiences. Of course, your delivery can be changed somewhat, but still, you will be speaking words that can't be changed. There still will not exist the spontaneity of telling a story.

The following is an authored story of mine. How would you approach presenting it differently (either reading or memorizing it) than you would a story you were going to tell?

THE SORCERESS

Martin liked to read. Already he'd read most of Mom and Grandma Schmidt's books. But there was one thing he didn't like. The dumb authors didn't know about kids. Martin was nine now, and when he read about nine-year-olds in the books Mom had, they either sounded like babies or like they were twelve years old.

Martin decided that maybe he'd be a writer when he grew up, and so, he could hardly believe it when Aunt Sarah wrote to say she was coming for a visit and was going to bring a writer with her, a woman who wrote books. It had never even entered Martin's head that he could meet someone like this.

They were to arrive on the second Saturday in November—if the weather was good. On Friday night, Martin peered anxiously between the lace curtains in the living room. He was afraid it would start to snow. He sat down on the couch and tried to read, but he couldn't concentrate.

The next morning he jumped from bed and ran to the window. The grass in the yard was frozen stiff like upside-down icicles.

He hurried into his clothes and ran downstairs. Mom was dusting the furniture because Saturday was cleaning day. He helped her move some of the furniture so she could mop the kitchen floor.

Then he looked out the front window. The frost had started to melt, and the sun shone brightly. He was glad. He sat down and picked up a comic book. It was *Captain Marvel.* He couldn't sit still.

His grandmother came in and sat on the couch. "Goodness, Martin, you're making me nervous," she said.

Martin came over and sat down beside her. "How did they meet?" he asked.

"Who?"

"Aunt Sarah and Miss Coleman."

"Well, she works at the library in Pittsburgh. She's a librarian."

"Do you think they're still coming?" Martin asked.

His grandma laughed. "Martin, if you don't stop asking, I think I'm going to go crazy."

All at once Martin heard someone on the front porch. He peeked out the window and saw Aunt Sarah's car. He hadn't even heard it. The woman with Aunt Sarah looked just like Martin thought she would. She was tall and thin, with hair that fell in waves nearly to her shoulders; black hair that glistened in the early afternoon sun. She wore a tan coat with fur on the sleeves and high-heeled black shoes.

Grandma opened the door. "Sarah," she said, "it's so good to see you." They hugged each other and stepped inside. Mom came in from the kitchen, drying her hands on a tea towel. Martin hung back, feeling shy now that the women had actually arrived.

"Hi, stinker," Aunt Sarah said. "How are you doing?"

"OK," Martin said.

"I'd like you all to meet Marie Coleman," Aunt Sarah said. Then she turned to the other woman. "Marie, this is my mom, my sister, Helen, and my nephew, Martin."

"Hi," Miss Coleman said and smiled.

"Let me take your coats," Grandma said. Miss Coleman wore a silky dress that went from a rusty brown color on top to a lighter shade on the bottom.

Once they were seated, Aunt Sarah said: "Martin writes stories too, you know. Don't you, Martin? He thinks maybe he wants to be a writer."

"Yes," he mumbled, not looking up. Why did Aunt Sarah say that? It made Martin's face feel hot.

"That's wonderful," Miss Coleman said.

Martin wanted to sink right through the floor. He wanted to die. He wished God would whisk him off the face of the earth.

"I'd love to read some of them," the woman continued.

Martin jumped up and raced through the kitchen and up the stairs to his room. He yanked open the middle drawer of his desk and pulled out crumpled sheets of paper.

Back downstairs, he thrust the papers at Miss Coleman.

"Thank you, Martin," she said.

He grabbed his jacket and ran outside to the front porch, leaning hard against the railing. He exhaled his breath from puffed cheeks. He stood there till his heart stopped pounding so hard. Then he sat in the old glider, cold against his legs and back. After awhile the front door opened. Aunt Sarah and Miss Coleman came out to the car and drove away.

They returned a few minutes later. Aunt Sarah went on inside. But Miss Coleman came up to Martin.

"Hold out your hands," she told him. He did as she asked. Into them she placed a book.

"You're stories are good," she said. The world seemed to have stopped, so Martin couldn't answer. "One day you'll be a writer. But you've got to work at it. You'll have to write every day, whether you want to or not. That's why I bought you this notebook."

Martin glanced down at his outstretched hands, at the thin notebook with its cover of blue, like marble. She squeezed Martin's arm. Then she turned and went inside. Martin went up to his room. He sat at his desk and started to write: "Once upon a time in a small town in Pennsylvania, a woman of magic came to visit a nine-year-old boy. She was a sorceress..."

Later that day the two women left, but Martin kept on writing.

KEEPING TRACK OF YOUR STORIES

Once you begin learning and telling stories, you need to get into the habit of keeping a record both of the stories and the presentations. You may want to keep either a journal or a card file.

You can list such things as the title, the author, the source, the type, the age group it's for, the time it takes to tell and any other useful comments. You might make a note of how the story can be adapted to a number of occasions and groups.

Along with all this information, you may find it helpful to record the first sentence or two to remind you how the story starts, the ending, the characters, and the sequence of events. This helps you recall the story; it refreshes your memory so that the effort of learning it isn't lost.

You can arrange the stories, maybe with cross references, by title, author, subject matter, age group, and so on. It's up to you to develop an exact method that works for you. Of course, you'll want to record where you told the stories and to whom, so if you ever go back, you won't duplicate what you've already done, unless you're asked specifically to do so.

Exercises

1. Choose a story in which you would use props, whether to show the audience how to do something or simply as an added dimension. Learn the story and present it.

2. Take an authored story, analyze it, and present it either as a reading or as a memorized piece.

3. Choose a story for telling and learn it. Experiment with recording it and with telling it to yourself in front of a mirror. Then tell it to friends and family.

4. Think about which way you'd prefer to present a story: telling it, reading it, or reciting it from memory? Can you see that each of these methods might be more appropriate for different situations? Think about what these situations might be.

5. Begin to develop a system to keep track of your stories so that you are certain you will not only remember them but the facts of their telling as well.

7. INTRODUCTIONS AND CONCLUSIONS

Introductions and conclusions serve the major purpose of transporting the listener and the teller to the realm of "otherness," where stories, for a time, are reality.

INTRODUCTIONS

What Purpose Do Introductions Serve?

Allow Audience to Get Ready

It is important, when appearing before an audience, to allow time for the listeners to become accustomed to you and the new situation that arises with your appearance. You should never plunge immediately into a story. There are times, of course, when it's all right to have little or no introduction. But even then, you should pause for a few moments before starting your story. This gives the listeners time to adjust psychologically and to tell themselves that something is about to happen to which they need to give their attention.

Set the Tone

Another important objective of an introduction is to set the tone for what is to follow. In most storytelling situations the audience has no idea what to expect. Exceptions, of course, would be at "tall tale" programs and the like, where everything is geared to one type of presentation. But this isn't usually the case. You have to give the audience clues as to what sort of story you will be telling, so they can get into the proper frame of mind.

How do you do this? Partly through demeanor and actions. If you were going to tell a serious story, you probably wouldn't bounce around or tell jokes beforehand. This would mislead the audience so that they would be in a different frame of mind. Then when you started the story, it would take even longer for them to adjust, and in all probability they'd either feel cheated or resentful.

Arouse the Audience's Curiosity

Besides simply gaining the audience's attention, you want to arouse their curiosity so they'll look forward to hearing the story. No matter what the situation, it's usually best to keep the introduction informal and on a personal level.

What Should an Introduction Include?

What about the actual content of an introduction? Obviously, there's no standard answer. It depends on you as a person, on the situation, and on the type of story. But whatever you say, you should keep it brief.

Relevance to Audience

There are certain things you may want to include. First, why are you telling the story? Maybe it's a tale you've liked for a long time. Maybe it's particularly relevant to your life or to interests of the audience.

Incidentally, remember that a story can be relevant for a variety of groups, depending on what you tell them about it. For example, in *The Best of the Story Bag*, Harlynne Geisler talks about a particular story, "The Wise Old Woman" from *The Sea of Gold* by Yoshiko Uchida. Geisler says the story can be used for "feminist audiences to illustrate an intelligent heroine who succeeds where men fail." It can also be told at retirement homes "because it is about a ruler who learns that old people are not useless." And "as a Japanese riddle tale," it can be used in a program of folktales from around the world. In this latter respect, it can appeal to "older children, families, or adults."

To aim your story at a particular group, your introduction would include something such as, "Of course, we all know that women are just as smart or even smarter than men. This is proved once again in this Japanese riddle tale, 'The Wise Old Woman.'"

To what diverse groups might you present the following story, and how would you change your introduction for each group?

THE HODJA AND THE BURGLAR

One night the holy but poor Hodja heard someone moving cautiously about his room, and, far from becoming alarmed, he cordially greeted the unknown and earnestly begged him to strike a light. The thief was so startled at this unusual request that he betrayed himself and asked in astonishment why the Hodja wished him to strike a light.

"Oh, fear nothing," said the Hodja in a reassuring tone. "I only wished to see your face that I might worship it, for truly you must be a very great man when you attempt to find in the dark what I am unable to find in the daytime, though I am constantly looking for it."

In the introduction you may state why you think the story will interest your audience. Maybe you can explain how you came upon a particular story and how it affected you. Maybe it's simply because you liked it so much that you want to share it.

Statement of Subject
Generally, a story should stand on its own, but don't always take this for granted. Sometimes a brief explanation may be necessary, but you shouldn't have to hammer home the point. Certainly, you should never give an abbreviated version of the story, either in the introduction or the conclusion. Since most often the stories you present probably will be your adaptations of other tales, you should do your best to make them clear in the telling. However, there's nothing wrong in unobtrusively stating that the story you are about to tell involves such and such. Then introduce the subject matter. Similarly, you might want to reinforce the theme in the conclusion.

CONCLUSIONS

The main thing to remember about conclusions is that you should stop when you are finished. Don't drag either the story or the conclusion on and on. Sometimes you may end by relating the story directly to the experience or interest of the audience. At other times you may end with a simple "Thank you." Whatever you say, it should be important or else remain unsaid. If you have nothing that needs saying, end with the story.

Sometimes the ending of a story is very strong and leaves no doubt of its conclusion. But sometimes it's difficult for an audience to know if a story has actually ended. This might be particularly true of nonsense stories. Then it's up to you to draw things to an end because the audience needs to feel some sense of completion.

Types of Conclusions

Rituals

Storytellers in other cultures sometimes have a saying that they either begin with or end with, and the audience expects this. You can do the same sort of thing by establishing your own "ritual" beginning and ending. To begin, it might be something as simple as sitting down and folding your hands, or it may be "calling over" the listeners to an "other" place, divorced from the everyday world: "Come with me to a far-off land where lies are but the truth, and truth are but lies." Any such announcement tells the listener the story is about to start.

At the end you may develop another set pattern that suits you. Or you may simply change positions, bow, or perform any other action that tells the audience you have finished.

Music

Another device that many tellers use to begin and end their stories is music, which can establish a particular mood. I once heard a storyteller who opened and closed her stories by playing a bongo drum. This device also can be used to accent any part of the story being told or to show transitions between scenes.

Music, rhythm, or even dance also can provide background color and accent important parts of the story.

Exercises

1. Plan an introduction and conclusion for the Japanese fairy tale "The Accomplished and Strange Teakettle," which appears on the next page.

2. Find and develop a story with which you can use music, either recorded or with an instrument you play.

3. On pages 129-134 are three different kinds of stories. Take the one you like most, adapt it, analyze it, do an introduction and conclusion, and find a place to present it.

THE ACCOMPLISHED AND STRANGE TEAKETTLE

A long time ago, at a temple in one of the eastern provinces, there was an old teakettle. One day, when the priest of the temple was about to hand it over the hearth to boil the water for his tea, to his amazement the kettle suddenly developed the head and tail of a badger. What an unusual kettle to come out covered all over with fur! The priest, thunderstruck, called in the novices of the temple to see the sight, and while they were stupidly staring and suggesting one thing and another, the kettle, jumping up into the air, began flying all about the room. More astonished than ever, the priest and his pupils tried to pursue it; but no thief or cat was ever half so sharp as this wonderful badger-kettle.

At last, however, they managed to catch it, and holding it with their united efforts, they forced it into a box, intending to carry it off and throw it away in some distant place so that they might be plagued no more.

But, as luck would have it, the tinker who fixed things for the temple stopped in. The priest suddenly thought that it would be a pity to throw the kettle away, and that he might as well get a trifle for it. So he brought out the kettle, which had got rid of its head and tail and had resumed its former shape, and showed it to the tinker. When the tinker saw the kettle, he offered twenty copper coins for it, and the priest was only too glad to close the bargain and be rid of his troublesome pot. Soon the tinker trudged off toward home with his pack and his new purchase.

That night, as he lay asleep, he heard a strange noise near his pillow. He peeped out from under his bedclothes, and there he saw the kettle he had bought, covered with fur. It had the head and tail of a badger and was walking about on four legs. The tinker started up in a fright when all of a sudden the kettle resumed its former shape.

This happened over and over again each night until at last one day the tinker showed the teakettle to a friend of his. "This is certainly an accomplished and lucky teakettle," the friend said. "You should take it about as a show, with the accompaniment of songs and of musical instruments, and make it dance and walk the tightrope."

The tinker, thinking this good advice, made arrangements with a showman, and they set up an exhibition. The fame of the kettle's performances soon spread about until even the princes of the land sent for the tinker to put on a show for them, and he grew rich beyond all his expectations. Even the princesses and the great ladies of the court took delight in the fur-covered, dancing kettle, so that no sooner had it shown its tricks in one place than it was time for them to move on to some other engagement.

At last the tinker grew so rich that he gave the now-famous kettle back to the temple, where it was kept on display as a precious treasure.

THE ROCK

Christ was walkin' 'long one day wid all his disciples, and he said, "We're goin' for a walk today. Everybody pick up a rock and come along." So everybody got their selves a nice big rock, ceptin' Peter. He was lazy, so he picked up a li'l bit of a pebble and dropped it in his side pocket and come along.

Well, they walked all day long, and de other 'leven disciples changed them rocks from one arm to de other but they kept on totin' 'em. Long towards sundown they come 'long by de Sea of Galilee, and Jesus tole 'em, "Well, let's fish awhile. Cast in yo' nets right here." They done like he tole 'em and caught a great big mess of fish. Then they cooked 'em and Christ said, "Now, all y'all bring up yo' rocks." So they all brought they rocks and Christ turned 'em into bread, and they all had a-plenty to eat wid they fish, exceptin' Peter. He couldn't hardly make a moufful offa de li'l bread he had and he didn't like dat a bit.

Two or three days after dat, Christ went outdoors and looked up at de sky and says, "Well, we're goin' for another walk today. Everybody git yo'self a rock and come along."

They all picked up a rock apiece and was ready to go. All but Peter. He went and tore down half a mountain. It was so big he couldn't move it wid his hands. He had to take a pinch-bar to move it. All day long Christ walked and talked to his disciples, and Peter sweated and strained wid dat rock of his'n.

Way long in de evenin' Christ went up under a great big old tree and set down and called all of his disciples around 'im and said, "Now everybody bring up yo' rocks."

So everybody brought theirs but Peter. Peter was about a mile down de road, punchin' dat half a mountain he was bringin'. So Christ waited till he got dere. He looked at de rocks dat de other 'leven disciples had, den he seen dis great big mountain dat Peter had and so he got up and walked over to it and put one foot up on it and said, "Why Peter, dis is a fine rock you got here! It's a noble rock! And Peter, on dis rock Ah's gointer build my church."

Peter says, "Now you ain't neither. You won't build no church house on dis rock. You gointer turn dis rock into bread."

Christ knowed dat Peter meant dat thing, so he turnt de hillside into bread and dat mountain is de bread he fed de 5,000 wid. Den he took dem 'leven other rocks and glued 'em together and built his church on it.

And that's how come de Christian churches is split up into so many different kinds: 'cause it's built on pieced-up rock.

AN HOUR IN PARADISE

In a small Jewish town, there once lived a shoemaker with his wife and their two children. He was very poor. A little straw roofed hut and a goat were all he owned. From sunrise to sunset the shoemaker worked at his bench mending shoes for everyone in town. He never complained however, and he thanked God every day for his daily bread. A gay tune accompanied by the rhythmic beat of his hammer could always be heard from his open window.

One day, a man, tall and slender, entered the shoemaker's hut. He had blue eyes that were cold and piercing and he was dressed like a rich Polish nobleman.

"I need a shoemaker on my estate," stated the nobleman. "I like you. If you will move to my principality I shall give you a fine home, a field and a cow, a servant, and a thousand gold coins a year."

"Are there any Jews in that region?" asked the shoemaker.

"No," replied the Polish count.

"In that case, I prefer to remain here," the shoemaker said.

The nobleman persisted and offered him more money, but the shoemaker stubbornly refused to accept any offer.

"What is it you want me to give you for your services?" the Pole shouted angrily.

"An hour in Paradise," answered the shoemaker.

The count was furious. He ran out of the hut, slamming the door behind him.

The shoemaker and his family were very busy the following day beautifying their home for the holiday of Shavuoth. They decorated the naked walls with green twigs and covered the floor with green grasses. After a festive supper, the family went to bed.

In his sleep the shoemaker dreamt that an old man with a white beard spoke to him, saying, "Go quickly to the window and look at the sky. It is about to split. Make a wish and it shall be granted."

The shoemaker rose from his bed and went to the window. A threadlike blue ray streaked across the sky and divided it into two halves. "An hour in Paradise!" the shoemaker called out.

The little hut was suddenly filled with light. Beautifully shaped leaves covered the twigs from which rare fruits hung. Birds of many colors flitted about, singing sweetly. The family woke up and sat spellbound listening to the song of the birds. An hour later everything vanished. All that was left of the shining hour was a handful of Paradise leaves on the bed where the children slept. The leaves had a most wonderful fragrance. The shoemaker's wife gathered them up and saved them.

Some time after then, an epidemic among the children broke out in town. The shoemaker's children became very ill. "I will give them a whiff of those wonderful leaves. Maybe it will help them," thought the mother. She brought the leaves to the children and as soon as they inhaled their fragrance they became well. News of the healing power of the wonderful leaves soon spread throughout the town. All the sick children smelled their fragrance and were cured.

The story about the remarkable Paradise leaves finally reached the palace where the count who owned this territory lived. His only child had also fallen victim to the epidemic and was about to die. The count sent for the shoemaker and the wonderful leaves. The child inhaled their fragrance and was restored to health.

The count was so grateful to the shoemaker for the gift of his child's life that he presented him with a deed to the entire town. And the shoemaker with his wife and children lived happily in this little town the rest of their lives.

THE THEFT OF A SMELL

In Paris, near the Petit-Chatelet rotisserie, in front of the baker's shop, a street-porter was engaged in munching a slice of bread, holding it in the smoke from the roasts and finding it, thus flavored, a very tasty tidbit. The baker permitted him to do this. But when the porter's loaf was all guzzled, the baker grabbed the fellow by the neck and insisted that he be paid for the smoke from his roast. The porter protested that he had not damaged the baker's goods in the slightest, that he had not taken anything that belonged to the other, and that, as a consequence, he owed nothing. The smoke in question was evaporating into the air and so was being wasted anyway. Moreover, it was an unheard-of thing in Paris for anyone to sell, in the street, the smoke that came from a roast. The baker replied that the smoke from his particular roast was not intended to keep street-porters from starving, and threatened, in case he wasn't paid, to knock the poor fellow's teeth out. The porter thereupon drew his cudgel and prepared to defend himself. The altercation grew, and the stupid Parisians came running up from all sides to see the fun.

It was then that old John the Fool, a citizen of Paris, happened along. When he saw the fool, the baker inquired of the porter, "Are you willing to have good old John here settle our dispute?"

"Holy Christ, yes," said the porter.

Old John, then, having heard their stories, directed the porter to take a piece of change from his belt. The porter put a Philip of Tours in the fool's hand. Old John took it and placed it upon his left shoulder, as though he were testing the coin's weight. Then he tapped it on the palm of his left hand, as though he were seeing whether or not it was counterfeit. Then he placed it over the ball of his right eye, as though to see if it were properly engraved.

While all this was going on, the silly mob stood silent, fully expecting a decision in favor of the baker, being certain that the porter did not have a chance. Finally, the fool rang the coin on the counter a number of times, after which, with a presidential majesty, holding his wand in his hand as though it were a scepter, he proceeded to jam his pointed, ape-faced, marten-skin cap with its ruffled-paper ears down over his head, gave two or three good preliminary coughs, and announced in a loud voice: "This court rules that the porter, who has eaten his bread in the smoke from the roast, shall be condemned to pay the baker with the sound of his money. And the said court further directs that each now return to his eachery, without costs and for just cause."

8. DELIVERING YOUR STORY

If you do not deliver your story well, you might as well not deliver it at all.

What is good delivery, then? Actually, as with so many things related to storytelling, there are no absolutes. Far from it, in fact. Everyone's style of delivery is different from everyone else's.

NERVOUS ENERGY

In any sort of performance atmosphere, you'll hear people talk about the importance of energy. A singer or actor can go on stage, worn out after a restless night, and come off feeling "charged up."

Performers are often told they need to keep their energy level up. What does this mean? Another way of describing it is by saying we become "psyched up." Just like any other performer, whether athlete or actor, the storyteller needs to anticipate, to be filled with excitement about the presentation.

The type of energy that makes us feel charged up is nervous energy channeled in a good direction. If it makes us feel exhilarated, then we have a much better chance of doing a good job in telling our stories. Channeled the wrong way, it affects us adversely and causes stage fright.

What Is Stage Fright?

Stage fright shows we are too concerned with self rather than with the story and its telling. We're thinking about how we might fail or make mistakes rather than remembering that we are only a channel for the stories we tell. And, yes, if we are too concerned with ourselves during a presentation, it will show in nervous habits or trembling voices and bodies. Certainly, we often can't help feeling stage fright, but there's one good cure. The more often we appear before an audience, the less the stage fright will affect us.

One of the reasons I like very much to perform in front of people is the "high" it gives me. I like that feeling, but believe me, when I first started performing, whether as a musician, actor, magician, or simply speech giver, I had stage fright so badly I shook. It took a long time to overcome it, but I finally did. I remember exactly when it happened, although I don't know exactly why. I was in a play, really frightened, exhibiting all sorts of nervous mannerisms. I looked out over the audience—more than a thousand people—and I thought, "You know, if any of those people could do what I'm doing right here at this minute better than I'm doing it, they'd be up here and I'd be down there." And it worked. Although I feel a rush of nervous energy any time I'm in front of a group, I almost never actually feel stage fright anymore.

CONTROLLING STAGE FRIGHT

Relax

One way to eliminate stage fright is to perform relaxation exercises just before you appear in front of an audience. There are any number of these, and I recommend taking a few minutes to do a few of them every time you're to tell a story.

The best exercises I've found involve stretching. Reach up as high as you can, and then reach higher, standing on tiptoe. Bend at the waist, jiggle a few times, and then hang limp.

I have two favorites. One is neck-rolls, which simply means you roll your head one way two or three times and then reverse direction. Be careful not to do this too often, or it will make you dizzy. The second exercise I always do is to stretch my right leg out in front, my left leg back, and *gently* bounce a few times. Then reverse legs and do the same thing again. For me, these two exercises, which take a total of perhaps sixty seconds, are all that I need to feel loose and relaxed. Here are a couple of other exercises I like. You may want to try them, in order to achieve the state of relaxed concentration desirable for storytelling.

1. Pretend your arms are ropes, uncoiled at the ends to form your fingers. Allow them to hang loose and then shake them. "Transfer" the tension from other parts of your body to the ends of your fingers. If your shoulders are tense, allow the tension to flow down the arms and wrists to the hands. Then shake it away as you'd shake dust from a throw rug.

2. Tense your feet and toes, then let them relax. Then try it with your stomach muscles, your shoulders and back, your thighs and pelvis.

Relaxation also can help you feel poised, so that you aren't easily rattled. There are other things besides the relaxation exercises that can help assure you'll do well.

Know Your Story

Most important, be certain you know your story. Knowing your story means that you've analyzed it, spent enough time learning it, and have presented it enough times to yourself and to friends to be self-confident about it.

Know Your Audience, Location, and Occasion

Second, as stated earlier, know as much as you can about the situation and the audience, so you won't have any nasty surprises you aren't prepared for, such as having to stop every minute or two while a plane flies overhead.

Be familiar with the occasion so what you plan fits in properly.

Be certain you're appropriately dressed. If it's an informal situation, dress neatly but don't overdress. If you wish, you can wear a "storytelling costume." Some storytellers I've known dress in rustic-type clothing to suggest that they come from a past age and that the oral tradition is a long one. Others dress in ethnic garb appropriate to their stories. A friend of mine tells Halloween stories to elementary school kids. She always wears a black witch's costume and carries lots of props, including a broom and a jack-o'-lantern.

Take Time to Ensure a Proper Frame of Mind

This, to me, is of top priority: Before you go in front of your listeners, take some time for yourself. I'm the type of person who needs quite a bit of time. When I'm presenting a program, I like to arrive at least thirty minutes beforehand so I can run through my stories in my head. This helps me get into a proper frame of mind, eliminating all outside interference.

Of course, like most people, I have worries and concerns. But I've trained myself to block these out or at least push them aside when I'm to appear in front of an audience. This is an absolute necessity if you want to do a good job.

I remember one time when I was appearing in a play and I'd just rushed my daughter to the hospital, where she'd been admitted with double pneumonia. This time I couldn't block out the worry. My performance suffered, with muffed lines and messed-up blocking. But in most cases, the worries aren't so extreme.

Even if you do get into the proper frame of mind where you can block out "internal noises," external things will still interfere. You just have to make the best of them, the same as you do if you forget part of the story. Actually, when you forget, you remind the audience that you're a human being just like they are. And you shouldn't feel embarrassed. Almost always the audience is rooting for you; they want you to succeed. Because of this, they're willing to overlook lapses and mistakes.

Be Sincere

Tell your story with sincerity. Tell it because you want to reach the audience. Because you like the story. Because you believe in what you're doing and know it's worthwhile.

HOW YOU LOOK AFFECTS YOUR DELIVERY

You tell the audience a great deal by posture and movement. Be certain that you convey what you intend to.

Body Language

I had an elementary school teacher who told one of my friends she had no idea what he meant when he shrugged his shoulders. Even then, I thought that was pretty dumb. Yet, until the last couple of decades, body language was pretty much ignored. Of course, we haven't come to the point where body language is admissible in a court of law, but we're getting closer. And why not? It's every bit as meaningful and in many cases more meaningful than oral language. Consider that mimes tell complete stories without using words; some people speak entirely in sign and body language.

Posture and Tone of Voice

The way we sit or stand and our tone of voice convey a great deal of meaning, usually not even on a conscious, thinking level. So, we need to make sure that one meaning does not contradict the other, unless it's meant to. You can't stand in front of a group of listeners, slouched over, arms folded protectively in front of your abdomen, and expect them to believe: "I'm happy to be here tonight to tell you one of my favorite stories."

Your posture should convey openness. You should appear relaxed (but not sloppy), friendly, and interested in what you're doing. If you show an audience you'd rather not be in front of

139

them, then they're going to show you by their restlessness, clearing of throats, and shuffling that they certainly agree with your message.

You can usually tell by a story's content that the verbal language contradicts the subtext or actual meaning. This is called **sarcasm**, or **irony**, which conveys the opposite of what the words themselves state. Knowing when to use sarcasm, then, is certainly another reason for understanding all the nuances of your story.

The most important thing to remember when telling stories is to be sincere about your presentation. Then you're much more likely to have the spoken and body language mesh. One should support, accent, and compliment the other.

Gestures and Movement

Gestures should appear natural. They should grow honestly out of the story you are telling and shouldn't appear planned, or again they'll convey a different message than you wish.

If you're comfortable with gestures, by all means use them. Some people simply can't help "talking with their hands." That's OK. It's only when the gestures are confused that the audience is confused. On the other hand, if you're uncomfortable with gestures, don't use them.

If you do use gestures, involve your whole body. People who are self-conscious often simply jerk the arm in one direction, without following through, or else they keep the gestures below waist level, so that they appear comical.

Basically, there are three types of gestures: *descriptive, directive,* and *emphatic.* The first type illustrates that something is this high, this wide, this big. Such gestures are easily recognizable in a particular culture.

The second type is the sort you use when you tell someone, "You go right down here to the corner, then turn left."

The third type of gesture is the one where you stamp your feet, pound on a table, and so on. All of these can add much to a story, as can movement from one place to another.

Generally, movement in the story is used when we change from one character to another or when we solve one complication and go on to another. We might also use movement that is characteristic of the protagonist and all the other important people in the story.

HOW YOU SOUND AFFECTS YOUR DELIVERY

Tips for Effective Voice Usage

Relax Your Throat

Just as you need a relaxed body when storytelling, it is essential that you have a relaxed throat. To relax tension in the throat, simply let the jaw fall open and produce an "ahhh" without paying attention to how it sounds. Remember how this feels and carry it over to more focused sound.

Generally, the more relaxed you are, the more fully you're using your resonators, the echo chambers or sounding boards in your body, and thus the more pleasant-sounding your voice.

Breathe Correctly

Particularly when speaking before a large group, you need to be sure to breathe deeply and let the air out in a steady flow. Many people, unfortunately, have a habit of shallow breathing, which is good when you're exercising—that is, running or jogging—but poor for speaking. You need to have better control of the air. When breathing from the chest, you simply aren't able to sustain a long sentence without squeezing the throat and thus risking laryngitis.

People usually breathe "correctly"—that is, they use the type of breathing needed for speaking—when they lie on their backs. Try this. You will see that your abdomen fills before your chest does.

Now stand up and see if you can breathe the same way. If not, then push as hard as you can against your abdomen and suddenly release the air. When you do this, your abdomen should quickly fill with air. Push the air out again, and let it rush back in. Keep practicing until this sort of breathing becomes automatic.

Don't Speak Too Fast

One common fault in voice usage that affects many people is speaking too fast. Often people aren't even aware of this. The best way of checking it is to record your stories. If you are going too fast (or too slow, which is not nearly so common), you can consciously try to alter your rate of speaking.

Don't Speak Too Softly

Another common problem is speaking too softly. Again, a recording of your storytelling should show you whether you're projecting enough.

Enunciate

Americans have the habit of sloppy speech—that is, they don't articulate distinctly. We say "Rida" for "Rita" and "watcha" for "what are you." Particularly in a performance setting, where you're telling a story to a number of people, you should speak distinctly without calling undue attention to the words. In a private conversation, if a friend can't distinguish the words, he or she can ask you to repeat them. Not so when you're telling a story to a group. To see how well you're articulating, again try recording your stories and listening to them, or have a friend listen closely to what you say.

Four Aspects of Voice Usage

You should strive for flexible voice usage in telling your story. This means taking into account time, volume, pitch, and vocal quality.

Time

One aspect of time is **rate**. In everyday life we naturally vary our rates of speaking, depending on the situation and the emotions we are feeling. Usually, when we're excited, we talk faster. When we're in a relaxed mood, we tend to speak more slowly.

During the analysis of your story, you should have figured out the emotional content and the particular emotions your characters are feeling. This should then translate partly into how fast or slow you tell these parts of the story.

Pausing is another aspect of timing. You already know how to mark pauses in your story. But for what reasons should you pause? One reason is to build suspense. You pause before an announcement of the winner or before one of the characters makes a decision either to save another's life or have him put to death.

Pausing also helps us understand meaning. It's a form of verbal punctuation. Sometimes it adheres to written punctuation; other times, it doesn't. For instance, if we paused in speaking for every comma, our stories would sound jerky. In the sentence, "I want to buy lettuce, tomatoes, celery, radishes, cucumbers, and salad dressing," it would serve no purpose to pause for commas.

On the other hand, you often want to pause where there is no written punctuation. For example, in the following story excerpt, you might use these pauses: "As to my philosophy of education, I firmly believe// the professor/ is always/ right. He is to be acknowledged// as the supreme/ being." The first and second pauses point up "the professor," while the third one emphasizes the word "right," also creating suspense as to what will be said. The pause after "acknowledged" both emphasizes and creates suspense. The final pause slows down the rate to add further emphasis.

Pausing also shows us meaning. For instance, compare "I'm going to have more bread.// Will you pass me some honey?" to "I'm going to have more bread.// Will you pass me some/ honey?" Or, "You're pretty/ tall/ and dark," to "You're pretty tall/ and dark."

Another aspect of time is **duration**. This refers to the length of individual sounds. Compare "Ow, I hurt myself" to "Owww, I hurt myself." Obviously, drawing out a sound or a word is a way of emphasizing it. You may way to mark this sort of thing on your copy as well.

Volume

Another means of emphasis or showing changes in emotion is to vary the volume. The higher the decibel level, generally, the more active the emotion. Also, of course, the larger the audience, the more loudly you have to speak. Individual words spoken at a higher decibel level show emphasis. For instance, in "What are you *doing*? Are you *crazy*? You'll get us into all *kinds* of trouble," the italicized words would be spoken more loudly than the others.

Pitch

If you varied the pitch in the same sentences, speaking the italicized words at a higher frequency level, that also would point them up. So pitch is another aspect of voice usage. Changes in pitch occur not only from word to word but within individual words. This is called **inflection**. Often a rising inflection conveys doubt, disbelief, or shock. In most cases you'd use a rising inflection to ask a question.

A falling inflection means such things as determination or certainty. But there are no exact rules; you need to experiment to see what works.

When learning and analyzing the story, you may want to indicate changes in pitch and inflection. Experiment with various ways of telling the story and mark down what you think is best. In the following, the lines closest to the word would be at a lower pitch.

"Oh, no!" Gordonov was horrified. "That isn't what I meant.

It's the opposite effect. To give up flight. Because I love you."

Vocal Quality

Another aspect of voice usage is vocal quality, or changes in the overtones of the voices. These changes can show differences in meaning, portray emotions, or show when a different character is speaking.

Most often quality is associated with mood and feeling or is changed to portray character. For instance, a whining quality suggests a dependent person who has failed to grow up.

Characterization

Changes in time, volume, pitch, and vocal quality can help differentiate between characters. Whether or not you actually impersonate the characters in your story, you probably will want to make some vocal changes to indicate a different character is speaking.

Certainly, the personality of the teller will affect the telling. What works for you might not work for someone else. Don't try to imitate other tellers or worry whether you're telling a story "correctly."

A storyteller should be heard and not seen. This the most important rule in storytelling. Emphasize the story, not the teller. The storyteller should be like a stereo or a radio. You can't separate the story from the device, yet the audience should not think about the device.

Exercises

1. Go through the following story, "Origin of the Medicine Pipe," to see where you might use different movement. What type of movement would be most appropriate?

2. In the story on page 150, mark the pitch changes you would use. Indicate the types of vocal quality, when this would change, and why.

3. Figure out how you would present the different characters in the story on pages 151-153. Mark both body and voice changes.

ORIGIN OF THE MEDICINE PIPE
by George Bird Grinnell

Thunder—you have heard him, he is everywhere. He roars in the mountains, he shouts far out on the prairie. He strikes the high rocks, and they fall to pieces. He hits a tree, and it is broken in slivers. He strokes the people, and they die. He is bad. He does not like the towering cliff, the standing tree, or living man. He likes to strike and crush them to the ground. Yes! Yes! Of all he is most powerful; he is the one most strong. But I have not told you the worst: He sometimes steals women.

Long ago, almost in the beginning, a man and his wife were sitting in their lodge, when Thunder came and struck them. The man was not killed. At first he was as if dead, but after a while he lived again, and, rising, looked about him. His wife was not there. "Oh, well," he thought, "she has gone to get some water or wood," and he sat a while; but when the sun had under-disappeared, he went out and inquired about her of the people. No one had seen her. He searched throughout the camp but did not find her. Then he knew that Thunder had stolen her, and he went out on the hills alone and mourned.

When morning came, he rose and wandered far away, and he asked all the animals he met if they knew where Thunder lived. They laughed and would not answer. The Wolf said: "Do you think we would seek the home of the only one we fear? He is our only danger. From all others we can run away; but from him there is no running. He strikes, and there we lie. Turn back! Go home! Do not look for the dwelling place of that dreadful one." But the man kept on, and travelled far away. Now he came to a lodge,—a queer lodge, for it was made of stone; just like any other lodge, only it was made of stone. Here lived the Raven chief. The man entered.

"Welcome, my friend," said the chief of Ravens. "Sit down, sit down." And food was placed before him.

Then, when the man had finished eating, the Raven said, "Why have you come?"

"Thunder has stolen my wife," replied the man. "I seek his dwelling place that I may find her."

"Would you dare enter the lodge of that dreadful person?" asked the Raven. "He lives close by here. His lodge is of stone, like this; and hanging there, within, are eyes,—the eyes of those he has killed or stolen. He has taken out their eyes and hung them in his lodge. Now, then, dare you enter there?"

"No," replied the man. "I am afraid. What man could look at such dreadful things and live?"

"No person can," said the Raven. "There is but one whom old Thunder fears. There is but one he cannot kill. It is I, it is the Raven. Now I will give you medicine, and he shall not harm you. You shall enter there, and seek among those eyes for your wife's and if you find them, tell that Thunder why you came, and make him give them to you. Here, now, is a raven's wing. Just point it at him, and he will start back quick; but if that should fail, take this. It is an arrow, and the shaft is made of elk-horn. Take this, I say, and shoot it through the lodge."

"Why make a fool of me?" the poor man asked. "My heart is sad. I am crying." And he covered his head with his robe, and wept.

"Oh," said the Raven, "you do not believe me. Come out, come out, and I will make you believe." When they stood outside, the Raven asked, "Is the home of your people far?"

"A great distance," said the man.

"Can you tell me how many days you have traveled?"

"No," he replied, "my heart is sad. I did not count the days. The berries have grown and ripened since I left."

"Can you see your camp from here?" asked the Raven.

The man did not speak. Then the Raven rubbed some medicine on his eyes and said, "Look!" The man looked, and saw the camp. It was close. He saw the people. He saw the smoke rising from the lodges.

"Now you will believe," said the Raven. "Take now the arrow and the wing, and go and get your wife."

So the man took these things, and went to the Thunder's lodge. He entered and sat down by the doorway. The Thunder sat within and looked at him with awful eyes. But the man looked above and saw those many pairs of eyes. Among them were those of his wife.

"Why have you come?" said the Thunder in a fearful voice.

"I seek my wife," the man replied, "whom you have stolen. There hang her eyes."

"No man can enter my lodge and live," said the Thunder; and he rose to strike him. Then the man pointed the raven wing at the Thunder, and he fell back on his couch and shivered. But he soon recovered, and rose again. Then the man fitted the elk-horn arrow to his bow, and shot it through the lodge of rock; right through that lodge of rock it pierced a jagged hole, and let the sunlight in.

"Hold," said the Thunder. "Stop; you are the stronger. Yours the great medicine. You shall have your wife. Take down her eyes." Then the man cut the string that held them, and immediately his wife stood beside him.

"Now," said the Thunder, "you know me. I am a great power. I live here in summer, but when winter comes, I go far south. I go south with the birds. Here is my pipe. It is medicine. Take it, and keep it. Now, when I first come in the spring, you shall fill and light the pipe, and you shall pray to me, you and the people. For I bring the rain which makes the berries large and ripe. I bring the rain which makes all things grow, and for this you shall pray to me, you and all the people."

Thus the people got the first medicine pipe. It was long ago.

THE TORTOISE AND THE EAGLE
by Aesop

A Tortoise, dissatisfied with his lowly life, when he beheld so many of the birds, his neighbours, disporting themselves in the clouds, and thinking that, if he could but once get up into the air, he could soar with the best of them, called one day upon an Eagle and offered him all the treasures of Ocean if he could only teach him to fly.

The Eagle would have declined the task, assuring him that the thing was not only absurd but impossible, but being further pressed by the entreaties and promises of the Tortoise, he at length consented to do for him the best he could. So taking him up to a great height in the air and loosing his hold upon him; "Now, then!" cried the Eagle. But the Tortoise, before he could answer him a word, fell plumb upon a rock and was dashed to pieces.

OLD GALLY MANDER
Journal of American Folk-lore

Once there was an old woman and she was so stingy she wouldn't spend a penny and she lived on ashcakes and water. She had a big long leather sack hanging up in the chimney with her money in hit. She didn't have any money 'cept gold and silver. So her hired girls got so they pilfered around and tried to find her money. So she sent her son over the ocean to get a girl who wouldn't know anything about her money. So he went and got her a girl that evenin'. And the girl fixed 'em the supper. So after supper the old woman wanted to go out a visitin'. So the old woman says, "Don't you look up the chimney." So of course as soon as the old woman was out of the house, the girl went and looked up the chimney and got to gougin' 'round with her stick, and directly the big long leather purse fell down and she looked in hit and seed the silver and gold and she just tuk hit and started out.

Directly she passed old cow. Old cow says, "oh come, pretty lady, milk my old sore bag."—"I've got no time to fool with your old sore bag. I'm going over the ocean." Went on a little way and met an old horse. "Oh come, pretty lady, wash my old sore back."—"I've got no time to wash your old sore back. I'm goin' over the ocean." Went on a little way, met a peach tree all loaded down to the ground with peaches. "Oh come, pretty lady, and pick off some of my peaches and rest my poor tired limbs."—"I've got no time to pick your old peaches. I'm goin' over the ocean."

Old woman come home, seed the girl was gone, looked up the chimney and seed her purse was gone, and just tuk out down the road a-hollerin', "Gally Mander, Gally Mander, all my gold and silver's gone and my great long leather purse." So she started off down the road at a loop-loopy-te-loop. Met the old cow. "Old cow, have you saw anything of a girl with a long leather purse?"—"Yes, run, old woman, and you'll soon overtake her."—"Gally Mander, Gally Mander, all my gold and silver's gone and my great long leather purse." Pretty soon met the old horse. "Old horse, have you saw a girl with a long leather purse?"—"Yes, old woman, and you'll soon overtake her."—"Gally Mander, Gally Mander, all my gold and silver's gone and my great, long, leather purse." Met the peach tree. "Peach tree, have you saw a girl with a long leather purse?"—"Yes, old woman, she's right down there at the side of the ocean."—"Gally Mander, Gally Mander, all my gold and silver's gone and my great, long, leather purse." And got to the ocean, caught her, flogged her up, and pitched her into the ocean.

Old woman tuk her purse, went back home, lives long time by herself. Then sent her son out to hunt her another girl away out where nobody didn't know 'em. So the girl come and the old woman liked 'er very well. After while old woman says, "Now, I'm goin' out to visit, don't you look up the chimney while I'm gone." So when she got out of sight the girl wanted to look up the chimney for curiosity. Got her stick, got to gougin' into hit, and directly the leather purse fell down. Looked inside and it was full of gold and silver, and she tuk out down the road. Directly she met old cow. "Oh come, pretty lady, and milk my old sore bag."—"I've got no time to milk your old sore bag, I'm goin' across the water." Went on, met the horse. "Oh come, pretty lady and wash my old sore back."—"I've got no time to wash your old sore back, I'm goin' across the water." Went on, met the peach tree. "Oh come, pretty lady, pick off some peaches and rest my poor tired limbs."—"I've got no time to pick off your peaches, I'm goin' over the water." So old woman come in, looked up the chimney. "Gally Mander, Gally Mander, all my gold and silver's gone and my great, long, leather purse." So she tuk down the road. Directly she came to old cow and said, "Have you saw a girl with a long leather purse?"—"Yes, old woman, and you'll soon over take her."—"Gally Mander, Gally Mander, all my gold and silver's gone and my great, long, leather purse." Directly she met old horse. "Old horse, have you saw a girl with a long leather purse?"—"Yes, run, old woman, and you'll soon overtake her."—"Gally Mander, Gally Mander, all my gold and silver's gone and my great long leather purse." Come to peach tree. "Pretty peach tree, have you saw a girl with a long leather purse?"—"She's right down by the side of the water." So the old woman shuck her and flogged on her and pitched her into the water. Then she tuk her long leather purse and went back home. "I'll stay by myself and eat ashcakes all the days of my life 'fore I'll bother with any other girl."

But atter a while, her son went 'way off where nobody didn't know 'em and brought her back another girl. Old woman, she jest stayed there and wouldn't go out un visit but atter a while she went out to visit. Says, "Don't you look up that chimney." So the girl tuk her stick and went to the chimney un gouged, un gouged, un directly the purse fell down. She opened it and it was full of gold and silver, so she grabbed hit up and started. She passed old cow. "Pretty fair maid, come milk my old sore bag." She says, "Yes, I'll milk your old sore bag," and she milked it and milked it. She passed the old sore horse. "Pretty lady, won't you bathe my old sore back?"—"Yes, I'll bathe your old sore back." She bathed it and bathed it. So she come to the pretty peach tree. "Pretty fair lady, won't you come pick off some of my peaches and rest my poor tired limbs?"—"Yes, I'll pick off some of your peaches." She picked un picked un picked. Peach tree says, "You climb up here in my limbs. The old woman ul be here in a minute."

Old woman come home, looked up chimney, seed her long leather purse was gone. "Gally Mander, Gally Mander, all my gold and silver's gone and my great long leather purse." She tuk out down the road. "Old cow, have you saw a girl with a long leather purse?"—"Yes, she passed here long, long, long ago and forgot abouthit."—"Gally Mander, Gally Mander, all my gold and silver's gone and my great, long, leather purse." Met old horse. "Old horse, have you saw a girl with a long leather purse?"—"Yes, she passed her long, long ago and forgot about hit."—"Gally Mander, Gally Mander, all my gold and silver's gone and my great, long, leather purse." Come to peach tree. "Pretty peach tree, have you saw a girl with a long leather purse?"—"Yes, but she's over the ocean long ago." Old woman, "What'll I do, what'll I do?"—"Go home and eat ashcakes all the days of your life." And that's what she got fer bein' so stingy.

BIBLIOGRAPHY

There are literally hundreds of sources for stories. Just look in any library for story collections, fairy tales, folk tales, tall tales, Bible stories and so on. You also can examine histories and biographies, as well as turning to your own family, either in stories they tell or in interesting ancestors. You can find ideas in newspapers and magazines. Actually, almost anything can provide a source for stories.

Following is list books on storytelling, which include many ideas for stories.

Barton, Bob. *Tell Me Another*. Markham, Ontario, Canada: Pembrok Publishers, Limited, 1986.

Bauer, Caroline Feller. *Handbook for Storytellers*. Chicago: American Library Association, 1977.

Bauer, Caroline Feller. *Handbook for Storytellers*. Chicago: American Library Association, 1987.

Breneman, Lucille, and Bren Breneman. *Once Upon a A Time: A Storytelling Handbook*. Chicago: Nelson-Hall, 1983.

Chambers, Dewey W. *Storytelling and Creative Drama*. Dubuque, Iowa: William C. Brown Company, Publishers, 1970.

Cook, Elizabeth. *The Ordinary and the Fabulous*. London: Cambridge University Press, 1976.

Cundiff, Ruby Ethel, and Barbara Webb. *Storytelling for You*. Yellow Springs, Ohio: The Antioch Press, 1977.

Livo, Norma J., and Sandra A. Rietz. *Storytelling Activities*. Littleton, Colorado: Libraries Unlimited, Inc., 1987.

_____. *Storytelling Process and Practice*. Littleton, Colorado: Libraries Unlimited, Inc., 1986.

Pellowski, Anne. *The Family Storytelling Handbook*. New York: Macmillan, 1987.

_____. *The World of Storytelling*. New York: Bowker, 1977.

Peterson, Carolyn Sue. *Story Programs: A Sourcebook of Materials*. Metuchen, New Jersey: Scarecrow Press, 1980.

Sawyer, Ruth. *The Way of the Storyteller*. New York: The Viking Press, 1962.

Schimmel, Nancy. *Just Enough to Make a Story: A Sourcebook for Storytelling*, 2nd ed. Berkeley: Sisters' Choice Press, 1982.

Shedlock, Ruth. *Art of the Story-Teller*. New York: The Viking Press, 1962.

Tooze, Ruth. *Storytelling*. Englewood Cliffs, New Jersey: Prentice-Hall, Inc., 1959.

Zuskind, Sylvia. *Telling Stories to Children*. New York: The H. W. Wilson Company, 1976.

ACKNOWLEDGMENTS

"The Winning of Dawn" as told by Charlie Sago from *Myths and Tales of the White Mountain Apache*, Grenville Goodwin, ed. Published for The American Folklore Society; New York: J. J. Augustin, Publisher, 1939.

"The Guilty Woman" from *Tales from the Basotho*, Minnie Postma, ed. Published for The American Folklore Society; Austin: University of Texas Press, 1964 and 1974.

Cassady, Marsh. "A Remembrance of Christmas Past," Chicago: *Aim Magazine*, Winter, 1988.

Cassady, Marsh. "Zepheriah and the Mighty Mini X," San Diego: *Writers' Haven Journal*, February, 1985.

"The Rooster Who Would Be King," as retold by Peninnah Schram, from *Jewish Tales One Generation Tells Another*. Northvale, New Jersey: Jason Aronson, Inc., 1987.

Geisler, Harlynne. "A Halloween Story / Paper Cutting: The Witch's House," from *The Best of the Story Bag*, 1988.

"The Accomplished and Strange Teakettle" from *Fairy Tales of the Orient*, Pearl S. Buck, ed. New York: Simon and Schuster, 1965.

"An Hour in Paradise" from *The Seventh Candle and other Folk Tales of Eastern Europe*, David Einhorn, ed. Hoboken, New Jersey: KTAV Publishing House, Inc., 1968.

Stories and Parables
—— *for Ministry* ——

from Resource Publications, Inc.

WINTER DREAMS and Other Such Friendly Dragons
by Joseph J. Juknialis
Paperbound $7.95
87 pages, 6" x 9"
ISBN 0-89390-010-9

This book of 15 dramas, fairy tales and fables dances with images that spark into clarity old and treasured principles. Discover the blessings concealed in "If Not For Our Unicorns" and "In Search Of God's Tracks." Especially good for retelling is the Advent story, "Sealed With A Dream."

WHEN GOD BEGAN IN THE MIDDLE
by Joseph J. Juknialis
Paperbound $7.95
101 pages, 6" x 9"
ISBN 0-89390-027-3

Here is fantasy adventure for young and old alike. In this collection of stories, find out what lies "Twixt Spring and Autumn" and "Why Water Lost Her Color". Meet Greta and Andy, whose mountain is "Carved Out of Love."

A STILLNESS WITHOUT SHADOWS
by Joseph J. Juknialis
Paperbound $7.95
75 pages, 6" x 9"
ISBN 0-89390-081-8

This collection contains 13 new stories, including: "The Cup," "The Golden Dove," "Bread that Remembers," "Golden Apples," "Pebbles at the Wall," and "Lady of the Grand." You'll find an appendix that tells you how to use the stories in church, school, or at home.

ANGELS TO WISH BY: A Book of Story-Prayers
by Joseph J. Juknialis
Paperbound $7.95
136 pages, 6" x 9"
ISBN 0-89390-051-6

A delight to read as a collection of stories, as well as a book well suited for use in preparing liturgies and paraliturgical celebrations. Scripture references, prayers, and activities that show how these story-prayers can be put to practical use in your church situation accompany most of the stories.

NO KIDDING, GOD, WHERE ARE YOU?
Parables of Ordinary Experience
by Lou Ruoff
Paperbound $7.95
100 pages, 5½" x 8½"
ISBN 0-89390-141-5

Gifted storyteller, Fr. Ruoff, helps find God for those who sometimes feel that he is hiding. These 25 stories work as effective homilies and are great for your planning — they are accompanied by Scripture references according to each season of the liturgical year.

THE MAGIC STONE and Other Stories for the Faith Journey
by James L. Henderschedt
Paperbound $7.95
95 pages, 5½" x 8½"
ISBN 0-89390-116-4

Share the word of Scripture in the context of today's lifestyles. These stories will make you want to read them aloud to let the word come to life for your congregation, prayer group, or adult education class. Readers and listeners alike are invited to think — about the "moral" of the story, about the story's significance in their lives, and about how this story can help their spiritual growth.

THE TOPSY-TURVY KINGDOM
More Stories for Your Faith Journey
by James L. Henderschedt
Paperbound $7.95
126 pages, 5½" x 8½"
ISBN 0-89390-177-6

21 stories that turn the ordinary world upside down and inside out. Use them for preaching — they're keyed to the lectionary — or in religious education. Your listeners will see themselves in the characters Henderschedt paints so vividly — perhaps in Jason, the bully from the title story, or in the two frail young people in "The Dance."

Fresh Storytelling in Ministry Ideas!

TELLING STORIES LIKE JESUS DID: Creative Parables for Teachers
by Christelle L. Estrada
Paperbound $8.95, REVISED & EXPANDED!
100 pages, 5½" x 8½", ISBN 0-89390-097-4

Bring home the heart of Jesus' message by personalizing the parables of Luke. Each chapter includes introductory comments and questions, an easy-to-use storyline, and discussion questions for primary, secondary, and junior high grades. Newly revised.

BALLOONS! CANDY! TOYS! and Other Parables for Storytellers
by Daryl Olszewski
Paperbound $8.95
100 pages, 5½" x 8½", ISBN 0-89390-069-9

Learn how to make stories into faith experiences for children and adults. Learn to tell about "An Evening With Jesus" and "From Hostility to Hospitality." Nine delightful parables plus commentary that shows readers how to tell the stories, how to use them in preaching and teaching, and how to come up with new stories.

Stories for Children

BOOMERANG and Other Easter Stories
by Fr. Chester Wrzaszczak
Paperbound $7.95
100 pages, 5½" x 8½", ISBN 0-89390-131-8
Allow Fr.Chester's Depression-era childhood stories to entertain you ten times over. This companion volume to his *St. Francis and the Christmas Miracle* brings about a bright, new Easter outlook. These ten stories will make you understand, through a child's experience, the solemnity of Good Friday and the joy of the Resurrection.

ST. FRANCIS AND THE CHRISTMAS MIRACLE and Other Stories for Children
by Fr. Chester Wrzaszczak
Paperbound $7.95
100 pages, 5½" x 8½", ISBN 0-89390-091-5
Inviting stories for adults and children written from a time when goodwill towards others, especially during Christmas, gave many a warm and renewed faith in man. Join Fr. Chester in recalling his Depression-era childhood, when money was scarce and what people lacked in money, they made up for in love and imagination.

PARABLES FOR LITTLE PEOPLE
by Lawrence Castagnola, S.J.
Paperbound $7.95
101 pages, 5½" x 8½", ISBN 0-89390-034-6
Be forewarned. When you pick up these stories, you risk being transformed. The language of children relays the message of these 16 powerful parables. Castagnola artfully reaches children in preaching, in teaching, and in the simple pleasures of storytelling.

MORE PARABLES FOR LITTLE PEOPLE
by Lawrence Castagnola, S.J.
Paperbound $7.95
100 pages, 5½" x 8½", ISBN 0-89390-095-8
Enjoy this companion volume to *Parables for Little People*. It gives you 15 imaginative children's stories with happy, positive messages. Find seven stories concerning the Gospel themes of sharing, caring, non-violence, and women's rights. Discover still other stories that retell Gospel stories—without mentioning the names of the original characters.

Stories for Growth and Change

BREAKTHROUGH: Stories of Conversion
by Andre Papineau
Paperbound $7.95
139 pages, 5½" x 8½", ISBN 0-89390-128-8
Here is an essential resource for RCIA, Cursillo, and renewal programs. You and your group will witness what takes place inside Papineau's characters as they change. These stories will remind you that change, ultimately, is a positive experience. You'll find reflections from a psychological point of view following each section to help you to help others deal with their personal conversions keyed to the lectionary.

JESUS ON THE MEND: Healing Stories for Ordinary People
by Andre Papineau
Paperbound $7.95
150 pages, 5½" x 8½", ISBN 0-89390-140-7
You know that everybody, at some time, needs to heal or be healed. Here are 18 Gospel-based stories that illustrate four aspects of healing: Acknowledging the Need, Reaching Out for Help, The Healer's Credentials, and The Healer's Therapy. Also included are helpful reflections following each story, focusing on the process of healing that takes place. Better understand healing, so that you, like Jesus, can bring comfort to those who hurt.

BIBLICAL BLUES: Growing Through Set-Ups and Let-Downs
by Andre Papineau
Paperbound $7.95, NEW!
160 pages, 5½" x 8½", ISBN 0-89390-157-1
Be transformed while you are deep into your own personal recovery. This book of biblical stories acknowleges the way people set themselves up for a let-down to come later. Papineau consoles us in revealing that Jesus, ever the playful one, often enters the scene to puncture a balloon, a deflating event that somehow leads to spiritual growth.